Connecting Libraries with Classrooms

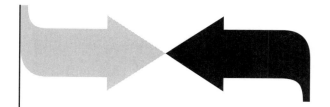

Connecting Libraries with Classrooms

The Curricular Roles of the Media Specialist

SECOND EDITION

Kay Bishop

 LINWORTH

AN IMPRINT OF ABC-CLIO, LLC
Santa Barbara, California • Denver, Colorado • Oxford, England

Library of Congress Cataloging-in-Publication Data

Bishop, Kay, 1942–
    Connecting libraries with classrooms : the curricular roles of the media specialist / Kay Bishop. — Second edition.
        p. cm
    Summary: "This book provides an in-depth exploration of the topics that are currently relevant in K–12 curricula, including the school librarian's role in dealing with these issues, collaborating with teachers, and connecting to classrooms"— Provided by publisher.
    Includes bibliographical references and index.
    ISBN 978-1-59884-599-0 (pbk. : acid-free paper) — ISBN 978-1-59884-600-3 (ebook)
1. School librarian participation in curriculum planning.   2. Media programs (Education)   I. Title.
    LB2806.15.B48   2011
    375'.001—dc22   2010051623

ISBN: 978-1-59884-599-0
EISBN: 978-1-59884-600-3

15   14   13   12   11   1   2   3   4   5

This book is also available on the World Wide Web as an eBook.
Visit www.abc-clio.com for details.

Linworth
An Imprint of ABC-CLIO, LLC

ABC-CLIO, LLC
130 Cremona Drive, P.O. Box 1911
Santa Barbara, California 93116-1911

This book is printed on acid-free paper ∞

Manufactured in the United States of America

Contents

About the Author

DR. KAY BISHOP is an associate professor at the State University of New York at Buffalo, where she teaches courses in school library media and youth services. She has also been a faculty member at the University of South Florida, the University of Kentucky, the University of Southern Mississippi, and Murray State University. Kay has over 20 years of experience as a school library media specialist at a variety of grade levels. She is the author of numerous articles, two books (*The Collection Program in Schools: Concepts, Practices, and Information Sources*, Libraries Unlimited, 2007 and *Connecting Libraries with Classrooms: The Curricular Roles of the Media Specialist*, Linworth, 2003). She coauthored two other books (*Staff Development Guide to Workshops for Technology and Information Literacy: Ready to Present*, Linworth, 2005 and *Inquiry-Based Learning: Lessons from Library Power*, Linworth, 2001).

Acknowledgments

I wish to express my sincere thanks to Rebecca Truelson, a graduate student at the State University of New York at Buffalo, for her assistance in locating articles and Web sites for this book.

Author's Note

At the American Library Association Midwinter Conference in 2010, the Advisory Board of the American Association of School Librarians (AASL) voted to use the official title "school librarian," rather than the previously adopted "school library media specialist" title. For the first edition of this book (2003) "school library media specialist" or "media specialist" was used in the title of the book and throughout the book. Whenever appropriate, I have used the term "school librarian" in this edition. However, there are chapters in which I am citing other documents or research that have used "media specialist" or "school library media specialist" so there are instances where I have used those terms. I, personally, am pleased to see a return to the use of "school librarian" as I found the other terms were not generally understood by lay people or educators, other than media specialists themselves. I advise the students in my library science courses not to be overly concerned about the title of the position or the name of the place ("media center," "library," or "learning resource center"). Rather I say to them, "Just do a great job of meeting the needs of the teachers and students in your school." In my opinion—"that is what it is all about."

Kay Bishop
Associate Professor
Department of Library and Information Studies
State University of New York at Buffalo

Introduction

The purpose of the second edition of this book is to provide school librarians with information and guidelines to help them assume active roles in the K–12 curriculum. School librarians need more than a surface knowledge of what areas of study are being included in the schools in which they serve. They should become acquainted with the learning standards for those areas of study and how the school librarian can contribute to helping students meet those standards. Librarians also need to understand special groups of students in a school, how the curriculum and the school are affected by the needs of those students, and how school librarians can help meet the needs of those students. Educational trends can have a tremendous impact on the curriculum of a school; therefore, it is important for school librarians to understand the trends that are being introduced into a school and the impact that a trend can have on the curriculum, on a school library program, and on the students in a school. Collaboration with teachers in specific subject areas, meeting needs of special groups of students, and becoming aware of educational trends are all important aspects of being actively involved in the curriculum of a school.

My primary reason for writing the first edition of this book was that I had not been able to locate a book that included all the areas mentioned above. Most library schools or education departments in universities that prepare professional school librarians have a course relating to the curriculum, but the textbooks used for such a course usually relate mostly to the instructional role of the school librarian. I received many comments from educators and students about my broader view of the role of the school librarian in the curriculum and was encouraged to write an additional book that could be used not only as a textbook for such a course, but also for staff development purposes, as several school districts indicated to me that they used the first edition for professional development in their schools. The book is not intended to be exhaustive. Instead selected topics are presented in depth, and then the reader is led to other topics that can be investigated.

Educators have also asked me how I use the book in my curriculum course. I have used the book for the past few years in both face-to-face settings and in an online version of the course. Students read a chapter from the book each week and take part in one or more discussion questions related to the topic. Then each student selects a topic from the lists provided at the end of each section or they may select a topic of their own choosing. They research that topic, using the "Learning More . . ." guidelines at the end of the section and write a research paper on their selected topic, as well as producing a handout that includes a few highlights from the paper and the role of the school librarian in relation to that topic. When the course is taught in a classroom setting, the students make oral presentations on the topics and provide all students in the class with handouts. In the online version of the course, the students' papers and handouts are posted (without identifying names), and the other students read the papers and handouts and then comment on them. Of course, I also include other topics in the course, such as the New York and AASL student learning standards, lesson planning, assessment, curriculum mapping, and research findings that relate to the topics covered in the book.

School librarians using the book as staff development have usually taken one chapter from the book and presented it to classroom teachers or other school librarians in professional development settings. One school district told me that their school librarians met and discussed one chapter from the book each month. The information in the book can definitely help practicing school librarians integrate library services into the curriculum.

Chapter 1 deals with collaboration with classroom teachers, administrators, students, and the community. Also, included are the new AASL *Standards for the 21st-Century Learner* and some of the legislation which affects school curricula. This chapter serves as a background for the remaining chapters of the book. This second edition of the book contains all new topics that are current and tend to provide interesting discussions. These chapters are part of three sections. In the first section three areas of the curriculum (reading in the elementary school, music in the middle school, and English as a second language in the high school) are discussed. The second section deals with three special groups of students (students with autism, students from highly mobile family backgrounds, and students with gay, lesbian, bisexual, or transgender orientations), all of whose needs are related to the curriculum. Three specific educational trends (Web 2.0, distance education, and inclusion) that impact the curriculum and the role of the school librarian are discussed in the last section. The "Learning More . . ." pages at the end of each section list other subject areas, special groups of students, and educational trends that can be investigated. Guidelines regarding how to obtain information on these topics are also provided.

Some chapters include a discussion of research related to the chapter topic. Additionally suggestions for extended activities are listed at the end of each chapter. These should be particularly helpful to instructors who wish to use this book as a textbook or to school librarians who want to obtain more information on a topic. Further readings and Web sites, which were carefully selected to provide additional useful information for each chapter topic, are listed in the Appendix. For the most part the Web sites include links that will lead readers to a wealth of practical information, including lesson plans for specific subject areas or groups of students.

It is my sincere wish that the second edition of this title is helpful to library educators, preservice school librarians, and practitioners in the field.

Chapter 1

Collaboration and Partnerships

I t is not surprising that the first guideline in the American Association of School Librarians' (AASL) *Empowering Learners: Guidelines for School Library Media Programs* deals with both collaboration and partnerships between the school media specialist and the learning community: "The school library media program promotes collaboration among members of the learning community and encourages learners to be independent, lifelong users and producers of ideas and information" (American Association of School Librarians, 2009, p. 19). *Information Power: Building Partnerships for Learning*, the national guidelines for school library media specialists in the United States published in 1998, also emphasized the importance of collaboration as it applies to a school's curriculum: "Today, as the library media specialist's role becomes even more closely linked with the curriculum, the significance of collaboration throughout the learning process is increasingly important" (p. 50). In order for school librarians to work effectively with others involved in the educational process it is essential that they have a clear understanding of collaboration and instructional partnerships.

Collaboration

Collaboration is a symbiotic relationship, but most often the school librarian needs to take the leadership in setting up collaboration with teachers, administrators, students, and the community. Although collaboration seems like an easy concept to understand, in reality it often proves difficult to implement in many schools. Unfortunately, preservice teachers and principals do not usually have clear perceptions or backgrounds from their university courses to help them understand the roles of school librarians or how librarians can be actively involved in the curriculum. Therefore, the school librarian needs to become an instructional partner and assume a leadership role in informing teachers, principals, and decision makers about the roles of the school librarian, particularly as they relate to collaborative efforts that affect the curriculum. In order to do this, the librarian must take time to establish good relationships with those persons with whom partnerships are important. Informing teachers, administrators, students, and parents of the services available in the school library is essential. The librarian must be interested in what teachers are teaching, become an expert on the curriculum goals of a school, and then provide recognizable links from the curriculum to the school library program. By encouraging collaboration and helping build effective teams throughout the school and community the school librarian can contribute to creating students who are independent lifelong users and producers of ideas and information.

Authentic Learning and Constructivism

While learning is the primary goal of all schools, educational reform has emphasized the importance of authentic, relevant learning. The focus of learning in today's schools has shifted from being teacher-centered to emphasizing student learning. While there are several types of learning theories that relate to authentic learning, one of the more popular educational theories in recent years is constructivism. The constructivist educational theory introduced in the late 1980s has been instrumental in the shift from teacher-centered to student-centered learning. In their book *In Search of Understanding: The Case for Constructivist Classrooms*, Jacqueline G. and Martin G. Brooks (1999) present five principles evident in constructivist classrooms:

- Seeking and valuing students' points of view
- Challenging students' suppositions
- Posing problems of emerging relevance
- Building lessons around primary concepts and "big" ideas
- Assessing student learning in the context of daily teaching (ix–x)

Much of the theory behind constructive learning is based on the work of Swiss developmental psychologist Jean Piaget, as well as on what has been learned in recent years about the development of the brain. Several Web sites can be found that deal with constructivism; some of these are listed in the Appendix.

Often schools that focus on constructive student learning assess students through performance-based projects, rather than traditional paper-and-pencil tests. During the projects, teachers serve as coaches or facilitators encouraging students in the use of critical thinking skills and the evaluation, organization, synthesis, and creation of information. While information itself is considered important in such learning, its use in problem solving is emphasized. Students are given opportunities to build on their own background and construct knowledge through their own experiences.

Constructivism and authentic, relevant learning work hand in hand, drawing from the same basic beliefs and principles that relate to students building their own new understandings through interactions with what they already know. School library media centers are perfect information-rich environments in which such learning can take place. However, authentic pedagogy and learning don't just happen; they require administrative support and collaborative planning between media specialists and teachers.

Inquiry-Based Learning

The first standard of AASL's *Standards for the 21st-Century Learner* (2007) notes that "Learners use skills, resources, and tools to inquire, think critically, and gain knowledge." With many U.S. schools being driven by the goals of the No Child Left Behind (NCLB) Act there has been a tendency for schools to teach to tests for accountability purposes, rather than fitting their curriculum to standards that focus on learning. Thus, it becomes a challenge for school librarians to implement learning standards that encourage inquiry, critical thinking, and collaboration. Yet most educators would agree that students learn best from well-designed curricula that support inquiry learning. Stripling (2008) notes that "inquiry is a process of learning that is driven by questioning, thoughtful investigating, making sense of information, and developing new understandings" (p. 50). School librarians can be instrumental in leading students through inquiry processes. Along with classroom teachers they can help students meet goals and standards that involve real-world problem solving and decision making. The school library should be a place of active research where students can be trained in methods of inquiry that help them seek knowledge and become better learners.

Connecting the School Library to the Curriculum

Information Power: Guidelines for School Library Media Programs (American Association of School Librarians & Association for Educational Communications and Technology, 1988), the first national standards and guidelines for media specialists in the United States based on qualitative rather than quantitative measures, emphasized the school library media program's contribution to the educational process: "The school library media program that is fully integrated into the school's curriculum is central to the learning process" (p. 15). In describing the media specialist's role as a teacher the document states: "The information curriculum is taught as an integral part of the content and objectives of the school's curriculum. . . . Library media specialists and teachers jointly plan, teach, and evaluate instruction in information access, use, and communication skills" (p. 39).

The extent to which the school library program actually becomes involved in the curriculum varies greatly across schools and school districts. In his book *Taxonomies of the School Library Media Program*, David V. Loertscher (2000) describes 10 possible levels of involvement, beginning with Level 1, which is no involvement, and moves progressively to Level 9, which is the mature library media center program that reaches the needs of every student and teacher who accepts its offerings in four programmatic areas: collaboration, reading literacy, enhancing learning through technology, and information literacy. Level 10 is curriculum development in which the library media specialist works with other educators in the planning and organization of what will be taught in the school or district (p. 17).

AASL's *Standards for the 21st-Century Learner* (2007) provides for school librarians ample opportunities to connect with the curriculum by partnering with classroom teachers to help students:

- Inquire, think critically, and gain knowledge
- Draw conclusions, make informed decisions, apply knowledge to new situations and create new knowledge

- Share knowledge and participate ethically and productively as members of our democratic society
- Pursue personal and aesthetic growth

Excerpted from *Standards for the 21st-Century Learner* by the American Association of School Librarians, a division of the American Library Association, © 2007 American Library Association. Available for download at www.ala.org/aasl/standards. Used with permission.

Information Literacy

As pointed out in *Empowering Learners: Guidelines for School Library Media Programs* (2009) information literacy has become a much more complex concept: "Information literacy has progressed from the simple definition of using printed reference sources to find information. Multiple literacies, including digital, textual, and technological, have now joined information literacy as crucial skills for this century" (p. 13).

Most school librarians have a fairly clear understanding of information literacy; however, many teachers and administrators do not understand the various facets of information literacy, nor do they understand the important role that school librarians play in the teaching of information literacy. The school librarian should work with classroom teachers to make certain that multiple literacies are embedded into curricular projects and lessons. Multiple formats, including emerging technologies, should be available through the school library, and students should be encouraged to critically think and use these formats to present data and information in useful ways (American Association of School Librarians, 2009). It is essential that school librarians, administrators, and classroom teachers work collaboratively to make certain students become information literate by gathering information, thinking critically, synthesizing information, and creating new knowledge.

Partnerships

The school and community contain numerous potential partners for school librarians. Each partner has its own unique needs, characteristics, abilities, and expectations, but the librarian will find these partnerships valuable, if not essential, to providing an effective program that supports the school curriculum (Farmer, 1999).

Instructional Partner with Teachers

As school librarians assume more and more teaching responsibilities in relation to information literacy and student learning, the instructional role of the school librarian is expanding. Recent AASL publications refer to this collaborative role as *instructional partner*. In *Empowering Learners: Guidelines for School Library Media Programs*, this role is described:

> The SLMS collaborates with classroom teachers to develop assignments that are matched to academic standards and include key critical thinking skills, technology and information literacy skills and cultural competencies. The SLMS guides instructional design by working with the classroom teacher to establish learning objectives and goals and by implementing assessment strategies be-

fore, during, and after assigned units of study. (American Association of School Librarians, 2009, p. 17)

School Libraries Work (2008) includes position statements from a variety of organizations, as well as empirical studies from 19 states and one Canadian province that cite the impact that school libraries and media specialists have had on student achievement. In that document the U.S. National Commission on Libraries and Information Science states the following:

> Today's library media specialists are important instructional partners or consultants in supporting and expanding existing curriculum. These specialists are working with teachers to change what is possible in the classroom and support exciting learning opportunities with books, computer resources, and more. (p. 4)

School librarians are in a unique position to be curriculum partners with classroom teachers since they work with all teachers and students in a school. However, in order to successfully do this, a librarian must know the curriculum, be acquainted with standards and guidelines in the various subject areas, and understand curriculum and instructional design. The school librarian will most likely have to take the leadership in such partnerships and look for opportunities to plan with teachers. However, experience has shown that once a school librarian has been successful in collaboratively planning with one or more classroom teachers, the word spreads and other teachers are more willing to seek out partnerships with the school librarian. Until that happens the librarian needs to remain steady in this proactive responsibility.

The ultimate instructional partnership with a classroom teacher involves collaborative planning in which a school librarian and teacher begin the planning process together, rather than having a school librarian look at a unit of study and then decide how to assist the teacher or integrate library skills into the unit. One of the biggest barriers in such planning is finding a common time for the librarian and the teacher (Bishop & Larimer, 1999). This is one of the reasons that flexible scheduling in a school library is so important. If classroom teachers and school librarians are to work together to ensure authentic teaching and learning in a curriculum, there must be time for planning and executing units of study.

Once a common time is established, it is important for the school librarian to learn the characteristics of students who will be involved (what are their grade levels, ability levels, learning styles, backgrounds, and interests in the topic of study?). It is also important to find out the planning and teaching style of the teacher, for this will vary greatly from teacher to teacher. After these two steps are accomplished, the process of planning objectives, needed materials, activities, and assessment can proceed. The standards (state, national, or both) that are addressed by the objectives should be prominently listed in the lesson plan.

The school librarian should also assume the role of information specialist during the planning so that the needed resources can be determined and linked to students' needs. It is always a good idea to plan far enough ahead so if resources are not readily available in the school library, purchase of materials or interlibrary loans can be utilized. Serving on curriculum committees and attending department or grade-level meetings will help the school librarian prepare for needed resources since often the topics for future study or incorporation into the curriculum are discussed at such meetings.

Having a written plan with responsibilities for each partner designated is essential for the success of collaborative planning. However, it is not necessary for each partner to be involved in every assignment of a unit. In some instances, both partners may also want to share some responsibilities. Figure 1 presents a form that can be utilized in the collaborative planning of a project. It can be adapted as needed. For instance, if the school librarian is planning with a team of teachers, additional space will need to be provided for the responsibilities of each member of the planning team. When the team plans an entire unit, goals for the unit need to be included and several of the forms will be needed—one for each assignment or project.

Principal

One of the most important partnerships a school librarian can have is with the principal. The principal is the primary decision maker in regard to the curriculum, educational reforms, personnel, and budgets—all of which impact the school library program and the role of the school librarian. As is true with teachers, school librarians may need to take the lead in forming partnerships with principals by making them aware of the services a professional school librarian can contribute to the school's curriculum. It is important that the principal understand the need for flexible scheduling and common planning time for the school librarian and classroom teacher. It is just as important, however, for the librarian to understand the principal's vision for the school so the librarian can align the library media program with the school mission (Donham, 1998).

The school librarian and principal have much in common since they both deal with all the teachers and students in the school, as well as with all the curricular areas. This commonality can serve as a building block for communication. Keeping the principal informed about what is happening in the school library through memos, e-mails, monthly reports, and scheduled short meetings will strengthen this communication and make it possible for the principal to assume some ownership in the school library program. Without this knowledge and ownership, it is difficult for a strong supportive partnership between the principal and school librarian to develop.

The principal also plays a key role in collaboration. In order for collaboration and teamwork to flourish in a school, the leadership of the principal is essential. It is amazing how quickly collaboration between teachers and a school librarian can occur when the principal supports and expects such collaboration in the school—and verbalizes that expectation with the teaching staff.

Students

Since students are obviously the focus of the learning process it is important to provide opportunities for them to participate in the planning of activities in the school library. When units of study are collaboratively planned by teachers and school librarians, taking time to obtain the input of students can help clarify directions for assignments and possibly provide additional ideas that could enrich the unit, making learning more relevant and interesting to the students.

The librarian can use the assistance of students in the selection of resources before and during a unit of study. Some students are particularly knowledgeable about Web

Figure 1

Collaborative Planning

Teacher/School Librarian: Grade Level:

Title of Project:

Description of Students:

Timeline:

Objectives:

Standards:

Resources Needed:

Instructional Activities:

Teacher's Responsibilities: School Librarian's Responsibilities:

Assessment of Student Learning:

Suggested Revisions:

sites and search engines that can be helpful in completing assignments. A school librarian should take every opportunity to use the expertise of those students who are skilled with the emerging technologies. They can be partners in helping teach information literacy skills to other students in a school. Also, simply asking students what resources they were not able to locate to adequately complete an assignment can provide a list of needed materials or resources that can be made available for future projects.

The Community

In a community there are numerous people with whom a school librarian will want to establish partnerships. When parents, school board members, volunteers, business people, and other citizens become informed about a school library, they will better understand how a library and school media program contribute to student learning. This, in turn, will produce verbal and fiscal support for the school library program.

A school librarian can be instrumental in helping parents become more involved in student learning by making presentations at school and community meetings about the selection of quality materials, including printed materials, computer programs, videos, and online resources. Such a presentation should also include how materials are selected for the school library since few parents are aware of the selection policies used in school libraries or the complexity of collection development (Donham, 1998). Additionally, the school librarian should be open to suggestions and input from parents in regard to materials and the school library program.

Writing articles about the school library program for school newsletters that go home to parents or are placed online is also an effective means of communicating with parents. If parent volunteers are needed in the library, this is an excellent place to make such information known, as is a short presentation at a PTA meeting. Parent volunteers can provide assistance to students, as well as informing others about the services of the school library. Treating parents with respect and rewarding their volunteerism with thank-you letters, small gifts of appreciation, or a volunteer luncheon will keep volunteers coming and, in turn, produce valuable advocates for the school library program.

Another important way to involve parents is to have them serve on a library advisory board. In this way parents become much more knowledgeable about the school library program and can serve important roles if there are material challenges made by parents or other members of the community.

Some schools open their library doors to parents and students during after-school hours or in the evening one or more times during the week, making it possible for parents and students to work together on homework assignments, examine the materials available in the library, and gain information literacy skills on computers or other technologies. Some school librarians and teachers collaborate to provide instructional programs to parents and students during such hours. These programs actively involve parents in student learning and also provide opportunities for parents to see how important the services of the library are to the school. Many school librarians develop Web sites on which they make online resources available to students and parents during after-school hours.

Informed parents can be one of the most valuable advocates for a school library program. Experience has shown that establishing positive relationships with parents is one of the most important partnerships a librarian can cultivate.

With tight education budgets in recent years many schools have also developed partnerships with businesses because of the economic support that businesses can provide. Furthermore, most businesses in a community have a genuine interest in quality education since their future employees are usually educated in the local school systems. Partnerships between businesses and schools provide opportunities for business personnel to learn about the school curriculum and programs.

The school librarian can be involved by partnering with businesses that can support the programs in the school library media center. Bookstores can provide discounts on materials for the school library or help sponsor an author visit. Often businesses are also willing to provide prizes, such as free pizzas, fast-food coupons, or books, for reading motivational programs sponsored by the school library. Other businesses have been willing to contribute to the technology needs of a school library by providing free equipment or software.

When working with a business partner, it is important to have a clear understanding between the school librarian and the business partner about the relationship. The librarian needs to make certain contributions made by a business are appropriate to the mission and objectives of the school, as well as to the school library media program. Standards should be set and followed so the integrity of the school library program is not in question. Many schools have policies that deal with business partnerships; thus, the school librarian should contact an administrator before setting up a school library/business partnership.

This type of partnership involves time, nurture, and accountability. Business partners want to be informed about the programs their contributions support and how those programs have affected student learning. In order to sustain such partnerships, a school librarian must be willing to take the time and energy to keep in touch with the business partner, show appreciation, and acknowledge publicly the contributions made by the business.

One of the most useful partnerships a school librarian can establish to help improve student learning is that with the public librarian. Unfortunately, many school librarians do not take the time to establish a relationship with a public library—even if the library is in close proximity to the school. In his research Callison (1997) reported public libraries had increased provision of services to young people, but school media specialists had not increased planning or networking with public libraries. Most public librarians are willing and eager to assist schools with programs and projects in which students are involved. Simply keeping the public library aware of upcoming assignments and changes in the school's curriculum is invaluable to students who may be using the public library in after-school hours. Some public librarians retain copies of student assignments so they can make certain they provide the materials that support those assignments. Having a large supply of materials on science projects and books that are on required reading lists are examples of how public libraries frequently help support the school curriculum.

The school librarian can publicize upcoming public library programs at school through flyers, announcements, morning news programs, and the school library media center's Web site. Some projects, such as reading incentive programs, can be planned and executed jointly by the school librarian and the public youth services librarian. Public librarians and school librarians are natural partners in student learning, but such a partnership requires communication. The school librarian may need to be proactive in setting up such communication by visiting the public library, making regular telephone calls, or suggesting a mutual lunch date, but in almost all cases an eager partner will be found at the public library.

Partnerships can also provide visibility and advocacy for the school library program. Without such visibility, people will not be aware of the importance of the school library media program to the curriculum and to student learning. Without advocacy, the school library program will not be sustained.

Conclusions

Collaboration and partnerships continue to be paramount to the success of school library media programs. The new national school library standards provide many opportunities for school librarians to connect their library programs to the curriculum. School librarians should strive to establish partnerships with principals, teachers, students, and the community, and then take active leadership in collaborating with all of these partners.

References

American Association of School Librarians. (2007). *Standards for the 21st-century learner.* Retrieved from http://www.ala.org/ala/mgrps/divs/aasl/guidelinesandstandards/learningstandards/standards.cfm

American Association of School Librarians. (2009). *Empowering learners: Guidelines for school library media programs.* Chicago: American Library Association.

American Association of School Librarians & Association for Educational Communications and Technology. (1988). *Information power: Guidelines for school library media programs.* Chicago: American Library Association; Washington, DC: Association for Educational Communications and Technology.

American Association of School Librarians & Association for Educational Communications and Technology. (1998). *Information power: Building partnerships for learning.* Chicago: American Library Association.

Bishop, Kay, & Larimer, Nancy. (1999). Literacy through collaboration. *Teacher Librarian, 27* (1), 15–20.

Brooks, Jacqueline Grennon, & Brooks, Martin G. (1999). *In search of understanding: The case for constructivist classrooms.* Alexandria, VA: Association for Supervision and Curriculum Development.

Callison, Daniel. (1997). Expanding collaboration for literacy promotion in public and school libraries. *Journal of Youth Services in Libraries, 11* (1), 37–48.

Donham, Jean. (1998). *Enhancing teaching and learning.* New York: Neal-Schuman.

Farmer, Lesley S. (1999). *Partnerships for lifelong learning* (2nd ed.). Worthington, OH: Linworth.

Loertscher, David V. (2000). *Taxonomies of the school library media program* (2nd ed.). Englewood, CO: Libraries Unlimited.

School libraries work (3rd ed.). (2008). Danbury, CT: Scholastic Library Publishing.

Stripling, Barbara. (2008). Inquiry: Inquiring minds want to know. *School Library Media Activities Monthly, 25* (1), 50–52.

Suggested Activities

1. Read one of the articles listed in the Appendix for Chapter 1. Write some reflections on what you learned from the article.

2. Interview several practicing school librarians and ask them questions dealing with their collaboration with classroom teachers. If some of the librarians have become particularly successful in collaborating with many classroom teachers, ask them how they manage the time commitment for such collaboration. Report your findings, including such items as the degree to which school librarians are collaborating, barriers to collaboration, and best practices for collaboration.

3. From Chapter 1 select one of the topics with which you are not very familiar. Research the topic and write a short paper on your findings. Suggested topics include constructivism, inquiry-based learning, the No Child Left Behind Act, or standards for school library programs.

4. Choose a partnership you would like to encourage (with a principal, teacher, students, parents, school advisory board, business, or a public librarian) and write a detailed plan of how you could develop such a partnership.

Subject Areas and the School Librarian

The most obvious role of the school librarian in the curriculum is collaboration with teachers in the various subject areas taught in the school. The number of subjects taught in schools has increased greatly from the traditional reading, writing, and arithmetic curriculum developed during the first half of the 20th century. Language arts, physical education, science, social studies, art, music, and computer science have become a part of the curriculum in most elementary schools. Band, orchestra, chorus, humanities, arts, and foreign languages are often added at middle schools, as well as sex and health education. Besides these subjects, a myriad of others are offered at high schools, including specialized science and math courses, drama, economics, psychology, business, and Advanced Placement and International Baccalaureate courses. Courses in family and consumer sciences, as well as career development and occupational studies, are taught in many school districts, beginning at the elementary school level and continuing through high school. It is no wonder schools have had difficulty providing quality education as the number of areas they are expected to include in the curriculum continues to increase.

Response to criticism about the quality of education following the 1983 publication of *A Nation at Risk* by the U.S. Department of Education's National Commission on Excellence in Education resulted in the development of national and state standards in almost all curriculum areas during the past few decades. Most states also initiated standardized testing programs based on state and national curriculum standards. These testing programs and the standards have had a huge impact on the K–12 curriculum.

If school librarians want to participate effectively in the curricula of today's schools, they must know what is being taught in classrooms. One of the best ways to do this is to participate in departmental meetings and serve on curriculum committees. Being able to collaboratively integrate information skills into the curriculum is one of the primary roles of school librarians. In order for the school library to serve as the hub of learning for the school, what goes on in a library must be closely related to the topics being taught in the classrooms.

The following section examines three subjects generally taught in schools—reading in the elementary school, music in the middle school, and English as a second language in the high school. All three of these subjects have experienced major changes in the past decade. Each chapter presents introductory information about the subject, including the national standards, trends, and controversies related to the subject. The last half of each chapter discusses ideas on how a media specialist can enrich the education of students in that particular subject, as well as collaboratively work with classroom teachers.

Reading in the Elementary School

Reading is the basis of our education; it is a foundation upon which learning builds (Killean, 2009). Thus, it is appropriate that much time is spent on teaching students to read in our elementary schools. Reading instruction has been controversial for decades, and educators, administrators, and policy makers have debated the best way to teach reading to young students. Numerous reading programs and national initiatives in both the U.S. and Canada have been touted as the most successful way to teach reading. Many reading programs have been tried, rejected, and in later years revived. In recent years emphasis has been on trying to increase the reading achievement of students, particularly on performance in the high-stakes testing that prevails in states since the enactment of the U.S. No Child Left Behind Act of 2001 (P.L. 107–110).

Standards and Assessments

The National Language Arts Standards were compiled jointly by the International Reading Association (IRA) and the National Council of Teachers of English (NCTE) in 1996. The standards were designed to prepare all K–12 students for the increasing demands of literacy. The vision guiding the standards is that "all students must have the opportunities and resources to develop the language skills they need to pursue life's goals and to participate fully as informed, productive members of society" (International Reading Association & National Council of Teachers of English, 1996, p. 3). In the preface of *Standards for the English Language Arts* it is noted that although the standards are presented as a list, they are, in fact, interrelated and should be considered as a whole. The following are the 12 English language arts standards:

Standard 1: Students read a wide range of print and nonprint texts to build an understanding of texts, of themselves, and of the cultures of the United States and the world; to acquire new information; to respond to the needs and demands of society and the workplace; and for personal fulfillment. Among these texts are fiction and nonfiction, classic and contemporary works.

Standard 2: Students read a wide range of literature from many periods in many genres to build an understanding of the many dimensions (e.g., philosophical, ethical, aesthetic) of human experience.

Standard 3: Students apply a wide range of strategies to comprehend, interpret, evaluate, and appreciate texts. They draw on their prior experience, their interactions with other readers and writers, their knowledge of word meaning and of other texts, their word identification strategies, and their understanding of textual features (e.g., sound-letter correspondence, sentence structure, context, graphics).

Standard 4: Students adjust their use of spoken, written, and visual language (e.g., conventions, style, vocabulary) to communicate effectively with a variety of audiences and for different purposes.

Standard 5: Students employ a wide range of strategies as they write and use different writing process elements appropriately to communicate with different audiences for a variety of purposes.

Standard 6: Students apply knowledge of language structure, language conventions (e.g., spelling and punctuation), media techniques, figurative language, and genre to create, critique, and discuss print and nonprint texts.

Standard 7: Students conduct research on issues and interests by generating ideas and questions, and by posing problems. They gather, evaluate, and synthesize data from a variety of sources (e.g., print and nonprint texts, artifacts, people) to communicate their discoveries in ways that suit their purpose and audience.

Standard 8: Students use a variety of technological and informational resources (e.g., libraries, databases, computer networks, video) to gather and synthesize information and to create and communicate knowledge.

Standard 9: Students develop an understanding of and respect for diversity in language use, patterns, and dialects across cultures, ethnic groups, geographic regions, and social roles.

Standard 10: Students whose first language is not English make use of their first language to develop competency in the English language arts and to develop understanding of content across the curriculum.

Standard 11: Students participate as knowledgeable, reflective, creative, and critical members of a variety of literacy communities.

Standard 12: Students use spoken, written, and visual language to accomplish their own purposes (e.g., for learning, enjoyment, persuasion, and the exchange of information).

Standards for the English Language Arts, by the International Reading Association and the National Council of Teachers of English, © 1996 by the International Reading Association and the National Council of Teachers of English, reprinted with permission.

Reading and NCLB

Under the No Child Left Behind Act (NCLB), which was passed by the U.S. Congress in 2001, each state is required to test for reading performance beginning in third grade and continuing each year through grade eight. The scores are used to determine adequate yearly progress (APY). Schools that do not make adequate yearly progress receive penalties that could even include state takeover.

The signature program of NCLB is the Reading First program, which focuses on putting proven methods of reading instruction into primary grades. Reading First is designed to help states, districts, and communities identify and adopt scientifically based reading programs, and ensure all classroom teachers (kindergarten through third grade) can identify children at risk of reading failure and provide effective early instruction.

Reading First's preschool counterpart is called Early Reading First and is designed to prepare children to enter kindergarten with language and literacy skills that will help them succeed in school.

Reading First uses the five-component model of reading that was recommended by panel members in the federally sponsored report of the National Reading Panel of 2000. Shanahan (2006) describes each of the five components:

- Phonemic awareness—the ability to hear and manipulate the individual sounds within words
- Phonics—how letters and sounds correspond to each other and how they can be used to decode or pronounce words
- Fluency—the ability to read text aloud with accuracy, speed, and proper expression
- Vocabulary—word meanings
- Comprehension—the act of understanding and interpreting the information within a text

Reading First is a state grant program that was created to encourage the use of scientifically based research as the foundation for K–3 reading instruction. As an incentive for schools, Reading First has $900 million in state grants, but states are only eligible for this federal money if they can demonstrate how they plan to help their local educational agencies improve reading instruction and student achievement using reading instruction and assessment built on scientifically based research. Programs funded under Reading First must demonstrate their capacity to comprehensively and effectively address all five of the components listed above (Scholastic, 2010).

Federal policies such as Reading First have put increasing pressure on schools to implement core reading programs. Core or basal reading programs are centered on one or more textbooks for each grade level that are called anthologies. Other components of the programs include phonics or decodable readers. CD-ROMs, DVDs, sets of library books, and workbooks are also sometimes available for purchase. Teachers are provided with teacher editions that contain recommendations for teachers' use (Brenner & Hiebert, 2010).

Some school districts are also using scripted curricula in keeping with the NCLB Reading First guidelines and their emphasis on phonics in reading instruction. These programs have scripted curricula that require teachers to read from a script while delivering lessons (Milosovic, 2007).

Other school districts have purchased electronic reading programs, such as Renaissance Learning's *Accelerated Reader* (AR) or Scholastic's *Reading Counts*. These computer software programs require students to take multiple-choice comprehension tests after they read books. The programs let the students know how many questions they have answered correctly, and the students are able to review the correct responses for questions that were answered incorrectly. The programs also keep track of the students' test results, as well as having the capability of diagnosing students' reading levels. Additionally, they can produce other types of reports, such as lexile (levels of reading) or zones of proximal development ratings for a classroom.

All of these programs (basal readers, scripted reading curricula, and electronic readers) have been very controversial with both teachers and school librarians. Research studies on the programs have not produced conclusive results on their effectiveness in improving reading skills.

Test Results

How well are these reading programs working in the United States? The 2009 National Assessment of Educational Progress (NAEP) reading assessment, administered by the U.S. Department of Education in 2008, showed that the fourth-grade reading scores were unchanged from 2007, but the average eighth-grade score was one point higher than in 2007. The percentage of fourth graders in the nation performing at or above the *Proficient* level increased from 29 percent in 1992 to 33 percent in 2009. The percentage of eighth graders performing at *Proficient* level in 2009 was 32 percent. The score gaps among racial/ethnic groups on NAEP reading continued for both grades 4 and 8 in 2009. Score gaps also persisted among other student demographic groups—between female and male students, public and private school students, and students who receive free and reduced-price school lunch and those who do not. In the fourth grade, for example, the average score of students in public schools was 15 points lower than the average score of students in private schools.

Scores indicate that there has been no overall gain in reading scores since the passing of NCLB. Billions of dollars have been spent on these programs. One of the goals was to eliminate racial and ethnic achievement gaps, but there have been no great leaps in this area. U.S. education secretary Arne Duncan commented on the 2009 test results:

> The reading scores demonstrate that students aren't making the progress necessary to compete in the global economy. We shouldn't be satisfied with these results. By this and many other measures, our students aren't on a path to graduate high school ready to succeed in college and the workplace. (Anderson & Turque, 2010)

Response to Intervention

Response to Intervention (RTI), a method of identifying and assisting students who are having difficulty learning, is being used in many school districts to help students who struggle with reading. RTI is not a new concept, but familiarity with the process and the term has increased greatly since the 2004 reauthorization of the Individuals with Disabilities Act. The purpose of RTI is not only to provide early intervention for students who are at risk for school failure, but also to develop more valid procedures for identification of students with reading disabilities. The Individuals with Disabilities Education Improvement Act of 2004 (IDEA) focuses on providing more effective instruction by encouraging earlier intervention for students experiencing difficulty learning to read. It also addresses the significant percentage of students whose reading problems place them in special education classes.

The National Association of State Directors of Special Education (NASDSE) includes three components in its definition of RTI: provision of quality instruction and interventions that are differentiated to meet student needs, collection of data over a period of time, and decision making that is based on the data (Nichols, 2009).

RIT uses a multitiered approach to assist students. The tiered model has three levels:

- **Level 1—Primary:** Data on students' progress is collected. A team discusses research-based interventions to be used by the classroom teacher for students who are having academic difficulty. The teacher provides the interventions, and progress is monitored and reviewed by the team.
- **Level 2—Secondary:** Children who continue to struggle are provided with more intense general education intervention, presumably in small groups.
- **Level 3—Tertiary:** Children who are still experiencing difficulty are placed in special education programs and their functioning is determined by their individualized education plans (IEPs). Special education teachers deliver the more intense instruction.

The hope of many educators and policy makers is that RTI will reduce the inappropriate placement of students into the learning disability category when their problem is that they were taught improperly in the early grades or could not keep up with the rest of the class (Gersten & Dimino, 2006).

Research

There is no dearth of research dealing with reading. The gamut of reading topics that have been studied is wide. Reading instruction, reading programs, reading interests, reading volume, reading motivation, reluctant and resistive readers, and reading and nonnative English speakers are just a few of the topics that can be found in the research literature. Because of space limitations, this chapter includes primarily a general discussion of reading instruction as it applies to elementary-age students, with emphasis on reading instruction and student achievement.

The reading wars that began over 30 years ago and continue today are basically between proponents of phonics (skill-based instruction) and those who advocate whole language (literature-based instruction). A teacher using skills-based instruction focuses on the relationships between sounds and letters. After students are able to recognize letters, they can then move on to word recognition and sight words. Students then are able to begin to process sentences and eventually paragraphs (Byrd, 2008).

Whole language advocates view reading as making sense of text. Contrary to the phonics perspective, students do not need to read every single word or letter to obtain the meaning. Whole language theorists see literacy emerging from a very young age, and they relate learning to read to learning to speak. Real literature, such as the children's books found in a school library, is used in the whole language approach. On the other hand, skills-based instruction generally uses a basal reader or other similar program created by a publisher specifically to teach phonics and other skills related to learning to read. Although there has been much research on both of these approaches, the majority of teachers support a balanced reading curriculum. Elementary teachers in Byrd's (2008) study did not see whole language and phonics approaches as diametrically opposed. They felt the reading programs in their schools were balanced and that having balance was an effective strategy for teaching reading.

The International Reading Association (IRA), a professional organization that promotes higher achievement levels in literacy, reading, and communication, sponsored a survey of 3,960 of its U.S. members to determine the effects of NCLB on its members. In the report findings Roller (2005) noted that most NCLB members agreed with the underlying assumptions of NCLB—that research-based instruction and professional development will improve student reading achievement. However, they did not think that severe sanctions for schools failing to meet adequate yearly progress would improve achievement.

The 2001 Progress in International Reading Literacy (PIRLS) study of reading achievement of primarily 10-year-old students in 35 nations found that the United States had the largest gap between literary and informational reading achievement of any nation in the study, with the gap favoring literary reading. In the 2006 PIRLS study, the gap narrowed somewhat, but average scores of U.S. students were statistically unchanged (Duke, 2010). This has resulted in studies in the United States relating to informational reading achievement, which have indicated that U.S. students struggle with comprehension of informational text as compared to narrative or literary reading. Duke (2010) notes that studies indicate that U.S. students have little experience with informational text in their early years of schooling. She calls for using real-world informational texts early in school.

Stephen Krashen, who is probably one of the most well-known researchers of reading studies, has analyzed and reported the results of numerous studies, including some of his own. Although the National Reading Panel in 2000 stated there was not sufficient evidence to support planned free-reading programs such as Sustained Silent Reading (SSR), Krashen has emphasized the importance of free voluntary reading for increasing reading achievement. Studies have shown that students who participate in planned free-reading programs, such as Sustained Silent Reading (SSR) or Drop Everything and Read (DEAR) do more independent, voluntary reading than students who do not participate in such programs (Nichols, 2009). Krashen states, "Only one method of improving reading ability really works: engaging in a great deal of interesting (better yet, compelling), comprehensible reading" (Krashen, 2009). He notes that studies indicate students who read more, read better, write better, spell better, have larger vocabularies, and have better control of complex grammatical constructions. He also states that one of the most convincing areas of research supporting this concept is that numerous studies consistently show that more access to books results in more reading (Krashen, 2004). Additionally, Krashen has shown that numerous studies have demonstrated that students who participate in intensive, systematic phonics programs do well on tests where they pronounce words out loud, but they do not do well on tests in which they need to understand what they read (Krashen, 2009).

In summary, the research seems to indicate that a balanced instructional program is needed to teach reading instruction in the early elementary grades. Each student is different, and teachers must be equipped to differentiate instruction to support the learning of each child (Borba, 2008). In addition, there needs to be a plethora of reading materials available, and students should have many opportunities to do independent reading.

The Role of the School Librarian

Reading is without doubt a discipline in which school librarians can make a huge impact. Motivating students to read has always been a primary role of librarians. Most elementary school librarians delight in opportunities to match the right books to students. School librarians read aloud to students, tell stories, conduct book talks, plan and implement author visits, sponsor motivational reading activities, lead book discussions, plan and conduct book fairs, and work cooperatively with public librarians to encourage participation in summer reading programs. School librarians also spend many hours selecting and processing the materials that are provided in school libraries to not only support the curriculum, but also to encourage students to read for pleasure. It is no surprise then that school librarians view themselves as partners with the findings and goals of Stephen Krashen's research—providing readers with interesting, comprehensible reading materials and motivating students to read.

AASL and Reading

A common belief noted in *Empowering Learners: Guidelines for School Library Media Programs*, (American Association of School Librarians, 2009) is that reading is a window to the world:

> Reading is the foundational skill for learning, personal growth, and enjoyment. The degree to which students can read and understand information in all formats (for example picture, video, print) and all contexts is a key indicator of success in school and life. As a lifelong learning skill, reading goes beyond decoding and comprehension to interpretation and development of new understandings. (p. 12)

In AASL's *Position Statement on the School Library Media Specialist's Role in Reading* (2010) the following roles of school librarians are emphasized:

- Providing a high-quality collection of reading materials
- Supporting print-rich environments that reflect the curriculum
- Organizing and promoting literacy projects and events
- Planning learning experiences that offer an interdisciplinary approach to literacy learning
- Partnering with classroom teachers, specialists, and other literacy colleagues to make decisions about reading initiatives and reading comprehension instruction
- Following an inquiry process to assess and use reading comprehension strategies
- Helping learners as they identify, analyze, and synthesize ideas and information by using a wide range of materials in a variety of formats
- Providing and participating in continual professional development in reading

Numerous pages on the AASL Web site are devoted to reading topics. One that is particularly beneficial to school librarians is the *School Library Media Specialist's Role in Reading Toolkit*, which contains a wealth of information including bibliographies, PowerPoint presentations, handouts, Web 2.0 tools, scenarios, elevator speeches, and self-assessments. The pages can be accessed at http://www.ala.org/ala/mgrps/divs/aasl/aaslissues/toolkits/slroleinreading.cfm.

Contributions to School-Wide Literacy

The school librarian's instruction in reading should be congruent with school goals and school-wide initiatives that address reading. Librarians should be especially active in school-wide reading promotions such as the Battle of the Books, the use of Sustained Silent Reading programs, or word-of-the day programs. If a school participates in the five pillar model of Reading First, school librarians can use some of the strategies suggested by Anderson (2009) to reinforce some of the pillars:

- **Comprehension Strategies:** directed reading, literature circles, KWL—What I Know, What I Want to Know, and What I Learned, paired reading
- **Vocabulary Strategies:** word walls, word cards, concept circles
- **Fluency Strategies:** readers' theater, read aloud, write and record podcasts
- **Phonics Strategies:** rhyming, teaching spelling patterns and word families
- **Phonemic Awareness Strategies:** ABC charts, making crafts to reinforce phonics

Betty Marcoux and David Loertscher (2009) asked the advisory board of *Teacher Librarian*, the professional journal that they edit, to help formulate a checklist of program elements that can help a school increase reading. A few recommendations that can be derived from the numerous items on their checklist are:

- A reading leadership team in a school should include the reading specialist, the school librarian, administrators, and classroom teachers.
- All faculty and staff should model lifelong reading importance to all students.
- Every student and teacher should receive information about new and innovative reading opportunities from the school librarian.
- Circulation policies should allow and encourage students to check out self-selected books, regardless of a book's level.
- Everyone in the school should be aware of the school-wide initiative and actively participate in it.
- The school library should serve as the hub of the entire reading program.
- Instruction of reading skills should go beyond decoding and fluency and should incorporate understanding and critical responses to texts.
- Time to read should be a daily part of the school day and beyond; time to read needs to include both required and recreational reading.
- A school's reading leadership team should promote collaboration with the public library on programs and reading opportunities.
- Professional development of all staff should include participation in activities that enhance school reading initiatives.

Professional Library

One of the most important services that a school librarian can provide to a school-wide reading initiative or to individual classroom teachers is to create a professional library of materials dealing with reading. Finding a cozy and comfortable spot in the library or in a room off the library and encouraging teachers to spend time there browsing the materials will help circulation of the materials. If a separate room is available, comfortable chairs, a pot of fresh coffee, some tea bags and hot water, and a plate of homemade cookies will make the area even more inviting.

Some of the materials that should be included in the area of the professional library are copies of reading research reports, language arts and information literacy standards, and current journal articles. If monies are available, subscriptions to some of the most popular professional journals, such as *Reading Teacher* and *Reading Research Quarterly*, should be available.

Numerous books dealing with reading instruction and motivation are available. Some of the titles that have been popular with teachers and school librarians include the following:

Allington, Richard. (2002). *Big Brother and the national reading curriculum. How ideology trumped evidence.* Portsmouth, NH: Heinemann.

Allington, Richard. (2003). *What really matters for struggling readers: Designing research-based programs.* New York: Addison-Wesley Longman.

Burke, Jim. (2000). *Reading reminders: Tools, tips and techniques.* Portsmouth, NH: Boynton/Cook.

Bush, Gail. (2005). *Every student reads: Collaboration and reading to learn.* Chicago: AASL.

Champlin, Connie, Loertscher, David, & Miller, Nancy A. S. (2005). *Raise a reader at any age: A librarian's and teacher's toolkit for working with parents.* Salt Lake City, UT: Hi Willow Research & Publishing.

Daniels, Harvey. (2002). *Literature circles: Voice and choice in book clubs and reading groups* (2nd ed.). Portsmouth, NH: Heinemann.

Daniels, Harvey, & Zemelman, Steven. (2004). *Subjects matter: Every teacher's guide to content-area reading.* Portsmouth, NH: Heinemann.

Follas, Alison M. G. (2006). *Reviving reading: School library programming: Author visits and books that rock.* Westport, CT: Libraries Unlimited.

Fox, Mem. (2001). *Reading magic: Why reading aloud to our children will change their lives forever.* San Diego, CA: Harcourt.

Gregory, Gayle, & Kuzmich, Lin. (2005). *Differentiated literacy strategies for student growth and achievement in grades K–6.* Thousand Oaks, CA: Corwin Press.

Harvey, Stephanie, & Goudvis, Anne. (2007). *Strategies that work: Teaching comprehension for understanding and engagement* (2nd ed.). Portland, ME: Stenhouse.

Jenkins, Carol Brennan, & White, Deborah J. D. (Eds.). (2007). *Nonfiction author studies in the elementary classroom.* Portsmouth, NH: Heinemann.

Johnson, Pat. (2006). *One child at a time: Making the most of your time with struggling readers, K–6.* Portland, ME: Stenhouse.

Krashen, Stephen. (2004). *The power of reading: Insights from the research* (2nd ed.). Westport, CT: Libraries Unlimited.

Marriott, Donna. (2002). *Comprehension right from the start: How to organize and manage book clubs for young readers.* Portsmouth, NH: Heinemann.

McGee, Lea M., & Morrow, Lesley M. (2005). *Teaching literacy in kindergarten.* New York: Guilford Press.

Miller, Debbie. (2002). *Reading with meaning.* Portland, ME: Stenhouse.

Pinnell, Gay Su, & Fountas, Irene C. (2007). *The continuum of literacy learning, grades K–2: A guide to teaching.* Portsmouth, NH: Heinemann.

Pressley, Michael, & Block, Catherine C. (2001). *Comprehension instruction: Research-based best practices.* New York, Guilford Press.

Routman, Regie. (2002). *Reading essentials: The specifics you need to teach reading well.* Portsmouth, NH: Heinemann.

Routman, Regie. (2007). *Teaching essentials: Expecting the most and getting the best from every learner, K–8.* Portsmouth, NH: Heinemann.

Sauerteig, Judy. (2005). *Teaching emergent readers.* Westport, CT: Libraries Unlimited.

Serravallo, Jennifer, & Goldberg, Gravity. (2007). *Conferring with readers: Supporting each student's growth and independence.* Portsmouth, NH: Heinemann.

Stead, Tony. (2006). *Reality checks: Teaching reading comprehension with nonfiction K–5.* Portland, ME: Stenhouse.

Taberski, Sharon, & Harwayne, Shelley. (2000). *On solid ground: Strategies for teaching reading K–3.* Portsmouth, NH: Heinemann.

Trelease, Jim. (2006). *The read-aloud handbook* (6th ed.). New York: Penguin.

Walker, Christine, & Shaw, Sarah. (2004). *Teaching reading strategies.* Westport, CT: Libraries Unlimited.

Wilhelm, Jeffrey D. (2002). *Action strategies for deepening comprehension.* New York: Scholastic Professional Books.

School librarians can keep a professional development collection current by asking teachers and other librarians for book title suggestions. Additionally, book reviews should be consulted in both library and reading journals, as well as online. Videos and DVDs can also be added to the collection. Sponsoring a summer professional reading club of classroom teachers and librarians is an ideal way to gather educators together to read and discuss professional books.

Conclusions

Reading instruction in elementary schools has been one of the most controversial topics in education for many decades. Many programs have been tried, rejected, and then revived again. In the past few decades the main debate has been between a phonics skill-based approach and a whole language approach. NCLB and the National Reading Panel Report have had heavy impact on reading instruction. However, the reading test scores since the passing of NCLB in 2001 have been disappointing. Research findings seem to indicate that the best ways to increase reading scores are through balanced reading programs that address the individual differences of students, providing time for and encouraging voluntary free-reading, and making certain there is a plethora of reading materials available to students in school libraries and classrooms. School librarians can play a huge role in supporting reading in elementary schools. Besides motivating students to read through a large variety of activities, school librarians collect and process materials that support both the curriculum and the reading interests of students. Additionally, school librarians can develop professional collections made up of high-quality professional materials that deal with reading instruction and motivation.

References

American Association of School Librarians. (2009). *Empowering learners: Guidelines for school library media programs.* Chicago: Author.

American Association of School Librarians. (2010). *Position Statement on the School Library Media Specialist's Role in Reading.* Retrieved from http://www.ala.org/ala/mgrps/divs/aasl/aaslissues/positionstatements/roleinreading.cfm.

Anderson, Cynthia. (2009). The five pillars of reading. *Library Media Connection, 28* (2), 22–25.

Anderson, Nick, & Turque, Bill. (2010). *Reading scores stalled under 'No Child' law, report finds D.C. fourth-graders a bright spot in disappointing 2009 data.* Retrieved from http://www.washingtonpost.com/wp-dyn/content/article/2010/03/24/AR2010032400929.html

Borba, Mary F. (2008). Literacy lessons on location. *Phi Delta Kappan, 89* (6), 440–441.

Brenner, Devon, & Hiebert, Elfrieda H. (2010). If I follow the teachers' editions, isn't that enough? Analyzing reading volume in six core reading programs. *Elementary School Journal, 110* (3), 347–363.

Byrd, Christy M. (2008). Reading instruction beliefs and practices of early elementary school teachers. *Psi Chi Journal of Undergraduate Research, 13* (2), 76–85.

Duke, Nell K. (2010). The real-world reading and writing U.S. children need. *Phi Delta Kappan, 91* (5), 68–71.

Gersten, Russell, & Dimino, Joseph A. (2006). RTI (Response to Intervention): Rethinking special education for students with reading difficulties (yet again). *Reading Research Quarterly, 41* (1). Retrieved from http://www.reading.org/Publish.aspx?page=/publications/journals/rrq/v41/i1/index.html&mode=redirect

International Reading Association & National Association of English Teachers. (1996). *Standards for the English language arts.* Newark, DE: International Reading Association.

Killean, Erlene Bishop. (2009). Yesterday, today, and tomorrow: Transitions of the work but not the mission. *Teacher Librarian, 36* (5), 8–13.

Krashen, Stephen. (2004). *The power of reading: Insights from the research* (2nd ed.) Portsmouth, NH: Heinemann.

Krashen, Stephen. (2009). Anything but reading. *Knowledge Quest, 37* (5), 18–25.

Marcoux, Betty, & Loertscher, David V. (2009). The role of a school library in a school's reading program. *Teacher Librarian, 36* (1), 8–14.

Milosovic, Sharon. (2007). Building a case against scripted reading programs. *Education Digest, 73* (1), 27–30.

National Assessment of Educational Progress. U.S. Department of Education. (2009). *The nation's report card.* Retrieved from http://nationsreportcard.gov/reading_2009/

Nichols, Beverly. (2009). *Improving student achievement: 50 more research-based strategies for educators.* Columbus, OH: Linworth.

Roller, Cathy M. (2005). *No Child Left Behind: A survey of its impact on IRA members.* Retrieved from http://www.reading.org/Libraries/Reports_and_Standards/NCLB_survey_022005.sflb.ashx

Scholastic. (2010). *An overview of Reading First.* Retrieved from http://www2.scholastic.com/browse/article.jsp?id=4562

Shanahan, Timothy. (2006). *The National Reading Panel Report: Practical advice for teachers.* Retrieved from www.learningpt.org/pdfs/literacy/nationalreading.pdf

Suggested Activities

1. Observe a primary elementary class during reading instruction. Write a report noting what you observed in relation to the approaches used. Was there more of a whole language or a phonics instructional approach or did it seem balanced?

2. Read several research studies on reading and summarize the findings in a paper.

3. Select a title from the list of professional books in the chapter and invite other people to read the book and join you in a book discussion group. Prepare some questions to use in the discussion.

4. Make an attractive handout, with at least one appropriate graphic, that focuses on the role of the school librarian in reading. Post the handout on the Web.

CHAPTER 3

Music in the Middle School

Any educator who has worked in a middle school setting is well aware of the wide range of physical differences, skills, and abilities of the students. The focus of the middle school student's social life often switches from family to friends. Middle school students have a strong need for acceptance by their peers. Many of the students have fragile self-esteems, and some may be cruel to those who are not in their accepted groups. Young adolescents are frequently beginning to question authority and are seeking independence; yet these same students also desire guidance and regulation.

When planning the music curriculum for a middle school, some of these characteristics of young adolescents should be taken into consideration. Since these students enjoy the company of peers and at the same time need to experience the respect of others, performing groups such as choir, band, or orchestra that require cooperation can be ideal for a middle school curriculum. However, since all students may not have the talent or interest in musical performance, other music courses, such as a general music class, need to be available for all students in a middle school. In such a course students can learn how to effectively listen to and appreciate music. Because music is an integral part of life, it should also be an integral part of the school curriculum.

Standards and Assessments

All music courses in the middle school should be grounded in the National Standards for Music Education, whose preparations were overseen in 1994 by the National Association for Music Education (MENC) Task Force on National Standards. The nine National Music Standards developed by the MENC Task Force encompass the major ways in which people interact with music in our culture. In 2007 the MENC Executive Board asked the task force to review the standards and to make any needed recommendations. Through the use of surveys the task force was able to obtain input from many music educators and practitioners, some of whom felt that the standards were unrealistically high. However, the task force noted that many of the states had used the national standards to create music standards for their states. Furthermore, many publishers of educational materials had developed materials that reflected the National Music Standards. The task force recommended revising the standards by developing achievement standards for each grade level (MENC Task Force on National Standards, 2007). The result of that recommendation is *The School Music Program: A New Vision*, which includes K–12 standards, prekindergarten standards, and what the standards mean to music educators.

The following are the nine music standards recommended by MENC for grades 5–8.

- Singing, alone and with others, a varied repertoire of music
- Performing on instruments, alone and with others, a varied repertoire of music
- Improvising melodies, variations, and accompaniments
- Composing and arranging music within specified guidelines
- Reading and notating music
- Listening to, analyzing, and describing music
- Evaluating music and music performances
- Understanding relationships between music, the other arts, and disciplines outside the arts
- Understanding music in relation to history and culture

From *National Standards for Arts Education.* © 1994 by Music Educators National Conference (MENC). Used by permission. The complete National Arts Standards and additional materials relating to the Standards are available from MENC: The National Association for Music Education, 1806 Robert Fulton Drive, Reston, VA 20191; www.menc.org.

The document also includes some meaningful comments about the standards as they relate to middle school students:

> The period represented by grades 5–8 is especially critical in students' musical development. The music they perform or study often becomes an integral part of their personal musical repertoire. Composing and improvising provide students with unique insight into the form and structure of music and at the same time help them develop their creativity. Broad experience with a variety of music is necessary if students are to make informed musical judgments. Similarly, this breadth of background enables them to begin to understand the connections and relationships between music and other disciplines. By understanding the cultural and historical forces that shape social attitudes and behavior, students are better prepared to live and work in communities that are increasingly multicultural. The role that music will play in the students' lives depends in large measure on the level of skills they achieve in creating, performing, and listening to music. (The National Association for Music Education, 2010)

Music educators and scholars have commented on how the national standards help address the difficult issues of educational quality and assessment. Gerrity (2009a) notes, "In this era of high-stakes testing and accountability, a quality-assured, standards-based curriculum may keep music off the chopping block and secure its good standings among education's core subjects" (p. 44). By employing standards-based curricula, music educators have shown that musical achievement exists and can be measured.

Music Education and NCLB

Much has been written about the impact of the No Child Left Behind Act (NCLB) on the arts. Smith (2009) writes, "It has become a mantra in education that No Child Left Behind, with its pressure to raise test scores, has reduced classroom time devoted to the arts (and science, social studies, and everything else besides reading and math)." Under NCLB, the arts are listed as a core academic subject. Because of its inclusion Susan Sclafani (2005), U.S. assistant secretary for vocational and adult education, states that "NCLB makes clear, the arts are a vital part of a complete education." She claims that the arts in NCLB are on par with the other core academic subjects and that NCLB defines what students should know and be able to do at various points in their schooling. In a conference call with 2,000 music education advocates, Arne Duncan, U.S. secretary of education, also defended the importance of the presence of the arts as a core subject in the Elementary and Secondary Education Act (ESEA), which was later reauthorized as NCLB. He noted that states and local school districts have flexibility to support the arts through federal title programs and U.S. Department of Education programs (DeHoff, 2009).

So if high-ranking government officials stress the importance of the arts in federal legislation, why are music educators and practitioners concerned about high-stakes testing and music education? NCLB does not require student testing for music or the other arts. They are not considered in the all-important adequate yearly progress (AYP) of schools, which is calculated by using the student testing results in reading and mathematics. Thus, many school districts have cut the amount of time in the curriculum for "specials" in order to allot more time to the tested subjects. Gerber and Gerrity (2007) echo the feelings of many educators when they state, "Let's not mince words here: the central culprit is the high-stakes testing environment shaped by ubiquitous statewide achievement tests and flavored ultimately by the punitive provisions of the No Child Left Behind Act of 2001" (p. 17). It is true that there seems to be a significant decline in music education in several states. In California there was a 50 percent decline in the percentage of students in music classes from 1999 to 2004. The greatest decline was in general music classes, which suffered an 85 percent decrease in student enrollment. During the same time period the number of music teachers declined by 26.7 percent. The reductions to music education programs in California were disproportionate when compared to all other subjects (Music for All, n.d.). A survey developed to study the impact of NCLB on music education in Ohio revealed that 43 percent of the music education programs were weakened since the passage of NCLB (Gerrity, 2009b). A similar type of situation exists in Illinois where middle school principal David Conrad (2006) states that school districts have cut fine arts and funding and in some cases have eliminated music and fine arts programs altogether. He goes on to say, "From my perspective as a public school practitioner, I believe that music education programs are in jeopardy nationwide" (p. 31). He also agrees that the widespread result of NCLB has been an assault on the untested subjects, such as music, the arts, foreign languages, and physical education, where each of these disciplines have suffered massive cuts and, in some cases, complete elimination.

Research

Tom Hone, the state superintendent of public instruction in Arizona, when discussing arts education and academic performance states, "If they're worried about their test scores and want a way to get them higher, they need to give kids more arts, not less. . . . There's lots of evidence that kids immersed in the arts do better on their academic tests (Smith, 2009).

Some of this evidence lies in research that has dealt specifically with music. Cobb (1997) examined ACT scores and the registration forms of 17,099 ACT test-takers, and he found that individuals who had taken two or more classes or activities in music had significantly higher ACT scores on the English, reading, and science subtests than students who were not involved with music activities or enrolled in music classes. Catterall, Chapleau, and Iwanaga (1999) tracked approximately 25,000 students over 10 years, with the results indicating that, regardless of socioeconomic background, secondary students involved in music had significantly higher standardized test scores, specifically in math, than students not involved in music. Butzlaff (2000) found a consistent correlation between reading ability and music instruction.

In four investigations (Miranda, 2001; Schneider, 2000; Trent, 1996; & Underwood, 2000) it was found that music participation was the only activity to correlate significantly with academic progress. Athletics or other extracurricular activities did not show similar results. The overall findings of research seem to indicate that there is a strong, reliable correlation between music and academic performance on standardized tests and other measurements of academic progress.

The Role of the School Librarian

The school librarian should first make deliberate efforts to provide plenty of materials to support the music curriculum in the middle school; additionally, the collection should contain books and other materials that match the personal musical interests of students. Materials about composers and musicians, music styles, musical instruments, and the music of various countries and cultures will most likely be needed to support the curriculum. In addition, materials that relate to pop culture and contemporary performers and bands are especially appreciated by the students. If funding is sufficient a CD collection should be considered; however, if the CDs are to be checked out both the students and teachers should be made aware of the copyright guidelines that apply to these materials.

Collaborative Activities

As high-stakes testing is emphasized more and more, the teachers of core subjects are often finding less time to collaborate with the school librarian. Because in many states the arts are not being included in their high-stakes testing, the opportunities for school librarians to collaborate with music and art teachers still exist. Such collaboration can provide many activities and projects that are of particular interest to middle school students, who most likely will welcome a chance to have breaks from classes where teaching to tests often seems to thrive.

Many successful examples of school library activities that can be planned and implemented in middle schools can be found in journals and on the Internet. A few of these activities are described below:

Rock and Roll: Joy Sibley (2001), a middle school librarian, worked with the teachers in her school on a large curricular project, with the theme of "changes." Sibley's interest in rock-and-roll trivia was used to develop lessons dealing with the history of rock and roll, the performers, and the actual recordings to which the students were able to listen. She talked to the students about how the music and the attitudes toward music have changed. Sibley even taught the students the dances from the rock-and-roll period, including the stroll, the jitterbug, the twist, the monkey, and the mashed potato. Sibley noted that students were fascinated and almost all of them tried out the dances.

Songs and Picture Books: Librarians Anna Rohn and Nancy Richards-Davis (2000) introduced seventh and eighth graders to picture books whose illustrators used the lyrics of songs. Students listened to the songs, wrote down the mood and images that came to mind as they listened, and then viewed the picture books that were based on the songs. In their art classes the students were able to make their own books, using assigned lyrics. Students learned how to complete a layout for the book pages and make beginning sketches for their illustrations. They also learned the basics of lettering and discussed the emotional effects of color.

Jazz: Joyce Adams Burner (2009) describes how to mix jazz into the curriculum by using jazzy materials in various grade levels. By tracing the history of jazz through biographies of singers and musicians, she notes that personal insights into race relations and social issues of the time can be shared. Her article in *School Library Journal* is packed with suggestions of books (both nonfiction and fiction), Web sites, and media (CDs and DVDs) that she claims will help young people dig jazz.

Ethics in Music: Valorie Xenakis (1999) describes a thematic unit on ethics and music, with the librarian, music teacher, language arts teacher, and technology teacher all collaborating. In the unit, students perform a portion of a copyrighted work of music without copyright infringement, gather information about composers, download a musical segment of a composition, and write biographical clues about a composer for a "Composer Clue" game. Throughout the unit the students learn from the school librarian copyright information relating to the activities in the unit. Students search the Internet and print reference materials to complete an ethical notes worksheet that deals with musical copyright infringement.

Other activities, either with or without teacher collaboration, can bring music to middle school students in the library. Some ideas that can be used by the middle school librarian include the following:

■ Make a bulletin board or display, using various quotes relating to music, such as Henry Wadsworth Longfellow's "Music is the universal language of mankind" or Paul Simon's "Music is forever; music should grow and mature with you, following you right on until you die."

■ Provide a display of musical instruments, including some unusual instruments, and have students research the instruments and place them in their traditional groups (string, wind, and percussion).

■ Have students watch various commercials on TV and analyze whether the music matches the commercial message.

■ Play music in the library before school and during lunch periods. Choose a different genre or time period each week and announce that genre on a bulletin board or daily school newscast.

- Work with a science teacher and have the students research the physics of various instruments (what makes the sound, how the sound carries, how to change the sounds). Have students demonstrate some of the findings.
- Work with a social studies teacher to explore the music of various cultures and listen to the folk songs from different countries or cultures.
- Work with a history teacher and a music teacher; have students research music from different time periods and make timelines of the various musical styles and instruments used throughout history.
- Ask a music teacher to make a list of leading musicians, composers or singers from the 16th century until the mid-20th century. In the library divide the students into pairs to do brief research on an assigned person. Have the students write their findings in short paragraphs that they read to the class. Explain that those persons were popular in their particular times. Then have the same pairs choose a musician from recent times, including pop culture musicians, and complete similar research, gathering information from both print and electronic resources. Ask the students to share their information about the contemporary musician and include a statement of why they think the person is popular today.
- Collaborate with a language arts teacher and plan a café event in the library where students read poetry aloud, listen to music, and partake of appropriate beverages and pastries.
- Invite musicians into the school library to discuss why they chose their careers. Then have students research various careers in music and share their findings.
- Bookmark Web sites on the Internet and take the students on tours of famous musical places, such as the National Music Museum, Music Museum of New England, Wesleyan University's Virtual Instrument Museum, the Virtual Museum of Musical Inventions, Carnegie Hall, the Rock and Roll Hall of Fame, and Graceland.

Music and Copyright

As mentioned in the above section, there are both legal and ethical copyright issues dealing with the use of music in K–12 schools. It is important for the school librarian to be aware of those issues and to make available information about them to both students and teachers. Information about copyright and fair use can be found in books, journal articles, and on the Web, but unless the person providing the information is a lawyer, it should be remembered that it is sometimes the author's best opinion that is being shared. There are, however, some guidelines that deal with music and are commonly expressed in writing, including those produced by the U.S. Government Copyright Office.

- Copying print music is not permitted except in emergency cases when purchased copies have not arrived in time for a performance. When the purchased copies arrive, they need to replace the emergency copies.
- Copies of purchased print music may be simplified, as needed for young learners, but the fundamental character of the work can not be altered and lyrics may not be changed or added.
- One copy of recordings of performances by students may be used for evaluation or rehearsal, and the teacher or school may keep the recording.

- A single copy of a sound recording of copyrighted music owned by the teacher or school may be used for the purpose of constructing "aural exercises" for examinations. All other copying of sound recordings is not permitted, even archival copies.
- Up to 10 percent of a copyrighted musical composition or recording may be reproduced for educational purposes only, but no more than 30 seconds of an individual recording.
- Recordings may not be physically or electronically combined or merged into teaching anthologies or compilations.
- All recordings must include the copyright notice.

Educators should be knowledgeable about the fair use guidelines that apply to copyright issues. *Fair use* is a legal principle that defines the limitations on exclusive rights of copyright holders and applies only to nonprofit educational institutions and homebound instruction. In order to claim fair use the following conditions must be met.

- The copy is used in a nonprofit educational institution or is used with homebound students.
- The copy is used in face-to-face instruction.
- The copy is used in support of curriculum objectives.
- The copy is legally obtained.

Copyright issues can be complicated, and it is always best to contact the school district's attorney if you have specific questions. You can also contact the person, publisher, or company holding the copyrighted material and request permission to use a piece of music. Two organizations, the American Society of Composers, Authors and Publishers (ASCAP) and Broadcast Music, Inc. (BMI) do most of the copyright clearances for professional music recordings so they can be contacted for copyright clearance (Simpson, 2001). Neither BMI nor ASCAP provides K–12 school licensing for music, in comparison to Movie Licensing USA, which provides K–12 schools and public libraries with a blanket license that covers public performances of many feature films (Harris, 2009). Both Simpson (2001) and Harris (2009) recommend purchasing clip art, music, and video that is sold expressly for student multimedia productions. Soundzabound, http://www.soundzabound.com/, is a good option for royalty-free music for schools. They have a large collection of music in many categories, provide CD and/or online access, and will take proposals for school district-wide and statewide licensing.

School librarians are not responsible for policing the activities of students or other library users for copyright infringements, but Russell (2005) suggests that the school librarian, after consulting with colleagues, might consider having students complete a copyright tutorial before having access to computers or signing a sheet whenever they use a computer. The school or school district should definitely have in place written procedures for possible copyright infringements. More complete information on all aspects of copyright can be found at the Web site of the United States Copyright Office, www.copyright.gov.

Conclusions

Time spent on music education in the curriculum of middle schools has declined over the past several years. Many music educators contribute this to the impact of high-stakes testing and NCLB. Researchers have studied the benefits of music education in secondary schools, and findings seem to indicate that music, as well as other arts, improves student academic performance. School librarians can help integrate music into the curriculum by working collaboratively with teachers on projects and activities that appeal to middle school students. Since there are copyright issues that relate to the use of music in educational settings, school librarians should make available to both teachers and students information dealing with copyright law and fair use.

References

Burner, Joyce Adams. (2009). Dig it. *School Library Journal, 55* (4), 45–46.

Butzlaff, Ron. (2000). Can music be used to teach reading? *Journal of Aesthetic Education, 34,* 167–178.

Catterall, James, Chapleau, Richard, & Iwanaga, John. (1999). *Involvement in the arts and human development: General involvement and intensive involvement in music and theater arts.* Retrieved from http://gseis.ucla.edu/faculty/files/catterall/catterall.involvement.pdf

Cobb, Ty Alvis. (1997). A comparison of the academic achievement of students who have a musical background (Doctoral dissertation, University of Mississippi, Oxford, 1997). *Dissertation Abstracts International, 58,* 11A, 4134.

Conrad, David. (2006). American music education: A struggle for time and curriculum. *Phi Kappa Phi Forum, 86* (4), 31–34.

DeHoff, Beth A. (2009). *Music for all news release.* Retrieved from http://www.docstoc.com/docs/16344258/Full-story—Music-for-All

Gerber, Timothy, & Gerrity, Kevin. (2007). Principles for principals: Why music remains important in middle schools. *General Music Today, 21* (1), 17–23.

Gerrity, Kevin W. (2009a). Enhancing middle-level general music: Suggestions from the literature. *Music Educators Journal, 95* (4). 41–45.

Gerrity, Kevin W. (2009b). No Child Left Behind: Determining the impact of policy on music education in Ohio. *Bulletin of the Council for Research in Music Education, 79,* 79–93.

Harris, Christopher. (2009). Copyright issues got you singin' the blues? *School Library Journal, 55* (10), 14.

MENC Task Force on National Standards. (2007). *October 7 report of the MENC Task Force on national standards.* Retrieved from http://www.menc.org/resources/view/october-2007-report-of-the-menc-task-force-on-national-standards

Miranda, Janet Young. (2001). A study of the effect of school-sponsored, extra-curricular activities on high school students' cumulative grade point average, SAT score, ACT score, and core curriculum subject grade point average (Doctoral dissertation, University of North Texas, Denton, 2001). *Dissertation Abstracts International, 63,* 11A, 3843.

Music for All (n.d.). *The sound of silence: The unprecedented decline of music education in California public schools.* Retrieved from http://legacy.musicforall.org/resources/advocacy/sos.aspx

National Association for Music Education. (2010). *The school music program: A new vision.* Retrieved from http://www.menc.org/resources/view/the-school-music-program-a-new-vision

Rohn, Anna, & Richards-Davis, Nancy. (2000). Songs in picture books. *School Library Media Activities Monthly, 17* (4), 12–13.

Russell, Carrie. (2005). Singing a different tune. *School Library Journal, 51* (3), 35.

Schneider, Timothy William. (2000). The effects of music education on academic achievement (Doctoral dissertation, University of Southern Mississippi, Hattiesburg, 2000). *Dissertation Abstracts International, 61,* 09A. 3429.

Sclafani, Susan (2005). *The arts are vital to young people's success in school and in life.* Retrieved from http://www.ecs.org/clearinghouse/62/36/6236.pdf

Sibley, Joy (2001). Rock and roll library. *School Library Journal, 47* (10), 41.

Simpson, Carol. (2001). *Copyright for schools: A practical guide* (3rd ed.). Worthington, OH: Linworth.

Smith, Fran. (2009). *Why arts education is crucial, and who's doing it best.* Retrieved from http://www.edutopia.org/arts-music-curriculum-child-development

Trent, Daryl Erick. (1996). The impact of instrumental music education on academic achievement (Doctoral dissertation, East Texas State University Commerce, 1996). *Dissertation Abstracts International, 57,* 07A, 2933.

Underwood, Evelyn Burnett. (2000). An analysis of the achievement patterns of high school students who participate in instrumental music and those who do not participate in instrumental music (Doctoral dissertation, University of Illinois at Urbana-Champaign, 2000). *Dissertation Abstracts International, 61,* 05A 1735.

Xenakis, Valorie (1999). Ethics in music performance projects. *School Library Media Activities Monthly, 16* (4), 15–17.

Suggested Activities

1. Read the articles in the Appendix (Chapter 3) and write some reflective comments about what is currently happening in music education classes in middle schools.

2. Send a message to a listserv of school librarians and ask them to share with you any ideas that they have used to include music in their school library programs.

3. Create a PowerPoint presentation on copyright issues that could be used as a professional development activity for music teachers or school librarians.

4. Develop a thematic unit on a musical topic. Include objectives, materials needed, and possible activities.

CHAPTER 4

English as a Second Language in the High School

One of the most significant demographic shifts affecting education in the United States is the increasing number of students whose primary language is not English (Callahan, 2005). A growing proportion of the enrollment of English language learners (ELLs) are in middle or high schools. Although 60 percent of ELLs in grades 6–12 still reside in five states (California, Texas, New York, Florida, and Illinois), other states have rapidly growing numbers of adolescent ELLs (Perkins-Gough, 2007). Between 1995 and 2005 more than 10 states experienced greater than 200 percent growth of ELL students, with Kentucky having the largest increase of 417 percent. By 2015 it is predicted that nearly one out of three students will be an English language learner (Christie, 2008). Even though the ELL population is growing throughout the United States, including in both suburban and rural areas, most ELLs reside in large urban areas. They are a heterogeneous population, with the majority of students having Spanish as their major language, but more than 450 languages are spoken by ELLs in the United States (Payan & Nettles, n.d.). Some of these students are new immigrants, but others were born in the United States. Researchers and educational policy makers have concentrated in the past on the education of elementary level ELLs, but there is a growing need to improve the literacy and academic skills of adolescents whose first language is not English.

Educational Challenges

Adolescent ELLs have dual challenges for they must not only learn how to communicate in English, but they also need to master complex academic content at the same time. It has been widely acknowledged that adolescent ELLs face multiple challenges, and a disproportionate number of them drop out of school (Derwing, DeCorby, Ichikawa, & Jamieson, 1999). The academic demands at the high school level make reaching parity with their grade-level peers increasingly difficult for English language learners (TESOL, 2006).

Whether high school ELLs are citizens, residents, or undocumented individuals, *Plyler v. Doe* ensures their right to an education in the United States. Unfortunately, many public school officials think there is little to gain by enrolling older adolescents in their schools so often these students are referred to adult literacy programs. According to the No Child Left Behind Act of 2001 (NCLB), after a year of enrollment in a school ELLs must take the state assessment tests, and their results must be integrated into a school's accountability measures. Thus, enrolling these adolescent ELLs often brings down a school's test scores and may put the school at risk of failing to make adequate yearly progress (APY). With increasingly limited school budgets, enrolling large numbers of ELLs in high school is often seen as a drain on available resources (Rance-Roney, 2009).

Many adolescent ELLs (57%) were born in the United States and are second-or third-generation residents (Batalova, Fix, & Murray, 2007). They may have achieved oral proficiency in English, but they lag behind in other areas of English literacy. The life circumstances of each individual adolescent ELL (high mobility, immigration status, native language, cultural difference from the U.S. culture, economic status) demonstrate the wide variety of challenges that these students bring to schools. Some of these students come to school with not only limited English, but limitations in their native languages, as well as poor academic backgrounds. Yet others may have very good academic backgrounds, and their primary barrier is not being able to communicate in English. Still others may come from traumatic situations in war-torn countries; thus they have additional emotional challenges. Schools must determine how to meet the needs of these individual ELL students.

Standards and Assessments

NCLB has focused particular attention on the language needs of ELLs by requiring each state to develop English language proficiency standards. While the previous two chapters listed national standards developed by national associations, standards developed by individual states for each area of the curriculum are particularly important. In most schools, teachers are asked to design their lessons to meet the state standards, rather than national standards. Thus, school librarians should be aware of the state standards in each curricular area and collaborate with classroom teachers to help the students meet those particular standards.

An examination of the state standards in the United States for English as a Second Language (ESL) or English Language Proficiency (ELP) reveals that most states address listening, speaking, writing, and reading English in their state standards. English intended for enjoyment, for analysis purposes, and for social interaction is frequently described in the various state standards. Sometimes specific cultural experiences are also addressed. Levels of proficiency are generally included and described in some detail. The terms used and number of levels, however, may vary. For instance, the levels might be beginning ESL, intermediate ESL, and advanced ESL. Students with no or very little understanding of English would be considered beginning level. As students gain understanding of phrases and sentences their level of proficiency would increase to intermediate, and finally they would reach an advanced level where they could express themselves fluently in various settings (personal, academic, social). Many states also have ESL standards for particular grade levels or groups of grades. In some of the state standards, such as those for New York and Tennessee, all the high school grades are lumped together, while in the Indiana standards each specific high school grade is addressed. Information about the ESL standards in a specific state can be found by using the keywords "ESL standards" or "ELP standards" and the name of the state. Often these standards are found on the Web site of the state's department of education.

World-Class Instructional Design and Assessment (WIDA) is a nonprofit cooperative of 19 states that published *The WIDA English Language Proficiency Standards and Resources Guide* in 2007. The publication includes five English language proficiency standards and levels of performance for different grade clusters (WIDA, 2007). Some of the states involved in WIDA use these standards in their individual states.

ELL students are required to take state tests in the content areas that are tested by their schools. Their test results are included in the accountability measures that must be reported to the state government. The validity and reliability of high-stakes testing that is conducted in English for ELLs are often questioned. The tests tend to reflect ELLs' English language proficiency, rather than content knowledge. Also, there are frequently test items that refer to ideas or events in the United States; thus ELLs who have not lived in the United States for long periods of time may not be familiar with the content of the test items. In some states accommodations are made for the ELLs taking the tests. For instance, they may be given additional time; take the test in a smaller setting, such as their ESL classroom; have questions translated into their native language; or be able to respond to the test items in their native language. The most common accommodations made for English language learners are those involving time and setting (Coltrane, 2002).

Teaching English as a Second Language

While there are schools that teach classes bilingually in two languages (generally English and Spanish), the majority of school systems today use a program referred to as teaching English as a Second Language (ESL). The main focus of an ESL program is to teach students the English language. Classes generally include students of different languages, and the instruction is done mostly in English. Secondary students in ESL programs most often spend part of the day in classes composed of all English language learners that are taught by certified ESL teachers and part of the day in mainstreamed classes. However, this varies from one school district to another, often depending on the number of ELL students and certified ESL teachers in a school district.

In the Monmouth-Roseville school district (District 238, a mainly rural and small town area in Illinois) there was only one ESL teacher for five schools when they began an English as a Second Language program in 2001. At that time there were 50 ELL students in the district, but the number of ELLs continued to grow, and the number of ESL certified teachers began to depend on the amount of funds available. In 2007, there was one certified ESL teacher at the one high school, and the primarily Spanish-speaking ELL students were often in classes that were taught totally in English. One of the ways that the district was able to bring up the grades and the attendance of ELL students in that high school was to require passing grades and attendance at both practices and school classes in order to be a member of the newly formed soccer team. Teachers in the high school also applied for grants to purchase textbooks and other materials for the ELL students. In addition, the district made efforts to build parent-faculty relationships. The teachers admit that they are not meeting all the needs of the ELL students but feel they are moving in the right direction (Geinosky, 2007).

Montgomery County, Maryland, located outside Washington, DC, is at the other end of the spectrum, with 26 separate high schools that enroll large numbers of ESOL (English for speakers of other languages) students. In 2008–2009, 9.4 percent (146) of Albert Einstein High School's 1,551 student population were ESOL students. They had an ESOL department that included seven ESL-certified teachers (one of whom was the department chair), one ESL-certified transition/academic intervention teacher, and three paraeducators. Additional ESL support came from two Spanish-speaking counselors, one of whom was solely dedicated to ESOL students, and a parent outreach specialist, who came to the school on a weekly basis to meet with parents. There were five instructional levels of ESOL classes offered (ESOL 1–5) and a special bridge English class for students who recently exited the ESOL program. In addition to the five levels of ESOL that were offered, Einstein also had a METS program (Multidisciplinary Education Training and Support). This program supported students identified as having "limited or no previous schooling or significant schooling gaps due to interrupted or disrupted education" (Lara Oerter & Elisabeth Wedam-Scott, personal communication, May 6, 2010).

Einstein's ESOL population is mostly comprised of Spanish-speaking students, but also includes students from several African and Asian countries. Two countries that are highly represented in the ESOL population at Einstein are El Salvador and Ethiopia. Special challenges faced by the ELLs at Einstein are the pressure to pass state-mandated High School Assessments (HSAs) in reading, algebra, U.S. government, and science after living in the United States for a short period of time. For those students who come to the United States with limited education or illiteracy in their native language, the challenge is tremendous. There is no vocational track available at the school because of the county's focus on academic achievement, although there is one such alternative technology school (Edison High School) that some students are able to attend.

Montgomery County allows ESOL students to remain enrolled in high school until they are 21 years of age, so students who are not able to meet graduation standards by the age of 18 can still continue to take classes for credit. With this law also comes the challenge of having 14-year-olds and 21-year-olds in the same classroom. Because the ESOL population at Einstein is so large, students often socially congregate with other ESOL students or with students who speak the same native language. This and cultural divides can inhibit ESOL students from developing relationships with students who are native to the United States. Social pressures include the necessity of working to support a family, as well as the temptation to be involved in neighborhood gangs. Students coming from war-torn countries sometimes struggle with psychological issues such as posttraumatic stress disorder. There are also dysfunctional family situations including reunification with students' parent(s) after 10 or more years of separation and physical or sexual abuse. Finally, students who begin learning a second language after puberty will often have more difficulty masking their native accent when speaking in English, particularly those from Asian backgrounds. This can sometimes be a cause for low self-esteem or lack of confidence when ESOL students are in their mainstream classes (Lara Oerter & Elisabeth Wedam-Scott, personal communication, May 6, 2010).

Another model of ESL education that has gained recent attention is used by some small public schools for immigrants in New York City. The model is sponsored by a New York–based nonprofit organization, The Internationals Network for Public Schools. Brooklyn International School, one of the international high schools, mixes immigrant students who possess various levels of English proficiency in the same classrooms. Teachers are assigned in groups of five to work with a cohort of students, and the teachers frequently work together on interdisciplinary learning projects. Professional development that addresses the needs of ELL students is a key aspect of the Brooklyn International model, as is the involvement of families as educational partners. The school emphasizes high expectations, along with effective support systems (Christie, 2008). Students report that they are not afraid to speak English in the school since all students are English language learners. The school has had a particularly impressive success rate with ELLs, with a four-year graduation rate of 65 percent in 2007, compared to New York City's overall four-year graduation rate of 26 percent for English language learners (Zehr, 2007).

ELLs in Mainstream or Inclusive Classrooms

Inclusion allows ELL students who are able to do so to participate in mainstream classrooms along with their English-speaking peers. One way of creating more inclusive settings for ELLs is to reach out to these students and learn about their cultures. Welcoming English language learners into a classroom with friendly gestures is an ideal way to begin communication with ELLs in the classroom. Klein (2008) recommends a learning environment in an inclusive classroom that contains anxiety-free learning situations, respect for each ELL's native language and culture, and many opportunities for success. O'Loughlin and Haynes (2004) note that alternative assessments for ELLs can be tried by mainstream teachers. Such assessments might include the following testing accommodations: reducing response materials for content area testing, providing a version of the test with simplified language, simplifying directions, reading test questions aloud, extending time to complete tests, allowing students to respond orally rather than in written form, and double grading ELLs' work (one grade for content and one for grammatical correctness).

A strong push to provide professional development on how to work with English language learners is being utilized in many school districts. ESL teachers can design and lead such professional development for the mainstream content teachers. Cho and Reich (2008) suggest some of the following techniques that can be shared with mainstream classroom teachers:

- Adjust speech rate and enunciation.
- Utilize visual aids.
- Introduce key vocabulary words.
- Provide information and directions in both oral and written forms.
- Connect students' prior knowledge to new knowledge.
- Break information into sequential steps.
- Create heterogeneous group work.

- Pair an ELL with an advanced ELL or native-speaking student.
- Think like a linguist and be mindful of the language being used in the classroom.
- Increase communication and collaboration with ESL teachers.

The use of educational technology for teaching ELLs has also been recommended by some educators and researchers. Including closed captioning when viewing television programs or DVDs can assist English language learners. Allowing ELLs to view online videos, such as those that can be found on the Discovery Educational Channel, can help reinforce the content in many subject areas (Carrigan, 2009). Other technologies that can be utilized with ELLs include audiobooks, authoring software, and educational computer games.

Unfortunately, many English language learners are enrolled in low-track curricula with a limited exposure to the content that is needed to enter higher education (Callahan, 2005). Even if they graduate from high school, the ELL students who are in the noncollege-preparatory curricula are not able to enroll in most colleges and universities. Second-language-acquisition research studies indicate that it takes five to seven years for most high school ELLs to achieve average grade-level performance in subject-area classes (Cho & Reich, 2008). Thus, providing more time to complete the requirements for graduation, as well as specialized support to adolescent ELLs as they are learning English, are possible alternatives to meet the needs of adolescent English language learners. Short and Fitzsimmons (2007) recommend an extended school year or day schedule, night and weekend classes, or simply a plan that makes it possible for late-entry adolescent ELLs to stay in high school for more than the expected four years.

The Role of the School Librarian

Students who are learning English bring a wealth of cultural experiences and languages to the schools in which they enroll. School librarians can capitalize on these human resources in addition to helping ELLs learn English and successfully adapt to school settings. It is vital that the school librarian create an ELL-friendly environment for students. Despite their age, some high school ELLs may have never been in a school library. Thus, they will need instruction on how to locate and check out materials, and where to return library materials. Understanding the Dewey decimal system is also vital to these students. This ideally can be done with collaborative lessons with ESL teachers, or if that is not possible, the school librarian can provide simple bookmarks that display the 10 Dewey categories, along with appropriate pictures that provide visual cues.

Signage is also important to ELL students so, if possible, it is good to translate signs into the students' native languages or include some visuals along with the signs in the library. The use of a translator for some languages may be needed in order to do this. Providing a handout of key vocabulary words that are used in a library setting will also benefit ELL students.

Literature

For the most part, the books and materials that are good for ELLs are also the same items that are good for other students in a high school library. Including many high-quality multicultural books in the collection and showcasing them often through displays and book talks will help ELLs realize that all cultures are respected and appreciated in a school. It is critical that a school library's collection contain current, relevant information about the predominant cultures in a school. These books can help newcomers value their cultural roots, as well as help native-English-speaking students gain respect and understanding of other cultures.

Both recreational and informational materials relating to various cultures need to be available in high school libraries. Primary sources of each of the world's major religions should be included in school library collections, as well as biographies of persons from various cultures. A good collection of world history materials and folktales from various cultures should also be a part of the school library collection. Providing materials with illustrations is particularly beneficial to English language learners. Audiobooks and magazines with numerous photos are especially appreciated by ELLs. Additionally, a collection of low-level, high-interest books can be an asset to high school ELLs; however, it is recommended that these books not have large type fonts or the appearance of young children's books.

Teaching with graphic novels to promote literacy is becoming increasingly popular in schools. Graphic novels can be especially beneficial in fostering the literacy needs of adolescent ELLs. School librarians should select graphic novels with substantive content, such as Art Speigelman's *Maus: A Survivor's Tale* (1986), which deals with the Holocaust and the struggling relationship between a father and son. These serious, substantive graphic novels can be used by classroom teachers to help teach about historical events, characters, and issues such as racism (Chun, 2009). Teens, however, want and need a good collection of recreational graphic novels, as well. For assistance in selecting graphic novels and illustrated nonfiction materials school librarians can access YALSA's *Great Graphic Novels for Teens* at http://www.ala.org/ala/mgrps/divs/ yalsa/booklistsawards/greatgraphicnovelsforteens/gn.cfm. Each year the Young Adult Library Association (YALSA), a division of the American Library Association, creates a list of recommended graphic novels and illustrated nonfiction for young people, ages 12–18. Numerous other Web sites also list recommended titles of this popular media format.

Technology

Technology offers many possibilities to adolescent ELLs. By using technology, students are able to have more responsibility for their own learning, while the classroom teacher and school librarian circulate among students, working individually or in small groups with students.

The use of technology can be helpful in teaching ELLs, but both practice and research have indicated that ELLs encounter some difficulties when searching for information on the Internet. The difficulties are not generally related to computer skills, but to the fact that the greatest part of the information on the Internet is written in English. School librarians can help ELLs become more successful in using the Internet by having students work in groups to conduct searches on the same topic in various ways—subject versus keyword or substituting various synonyms. In such activities ELL students have opportunities to use their language skills, as well as their critical thinking skills. They will also learn new vocabulary words as they conduct the searches.

School librarians can utilize online text and interactive whiteboards to help groups of English language learners focus together on one element of a lesson. Videostreaming is another high-tech tool that can be used in the school library to introduce or reinforce material visually.

Rethinking the use of popular technology devices and using them for educational purposes are excellent ways to motivate secondary ELLs to learn English. In 2004, a school librarian in a New Jersey middle school used technology creatively by requesting funds from district school officials to purchase 23 iPods for an after-school bilingual (English/Spanish) program. She downloaded songs that she thought would appeal to the students and typed out the lyrics. By deleting the nouns from the lyrics, and then later the verbs and adjectives, the students had to fill in the missing words and learn the meaning of the lyrics. The librarian also downloaded audiobooks and then added recording devices to the iPods so the ELLs could listen to their pronunciation as they talked to one another and read poetry. The Pod People Program was so popular that it was added to the regular school schedule, and in 2007 school officials decided to add the program to other schools in the district (Hu, 2007).

Chun (2009) notes that students are becoming increasingly oriented toward information delivered through online media. Librarians, as well as teachers, should create lessons and experiences that integrate technology into ELLs' learning. Adolescent English language learners also need opportunities to be more than passive receivers of knowledge; with the assistance of new technologies, they can become active producers of information.

Conclusions

The number of adolescent English language learners in schools is increasing each year, presenting numerous challenges in U.S. high school education. High-stakes testing required by NCLB has resulted in ELLs' test scores being integrated into a school's progress scores. The validity and reliability of these tests, which are conducted in English, have been questioned by many educators. Instruction for ELLs in either self-contained classrooms or mainstreamed classes can be improved by using specific strategies, such as breaking information into small sequential steps, using visual aids, and explaining key vocabulary words. School librarians need to create ELL-friendly environments where English language learners are welcomed and are able to locate materials that help them learn English and adapt to school. New technologies can be used in both the school library and classrooms to motivate adolescent ELLs to gain the information that they need to succeed in and beyond high school.

References

Batalova, Jean, Fix, Michael, & Murray, Julie. (2007). *Measures of change: The demography and literacy of adolescent learners—A report to the Carnegie Corporation of New York:* Washington, DC: Migration Policy Institute.

Callahan, Rebecca M. (2005). Tracking and high school English learners: Limiting opportunity to learn. *American Education Research Journal, 42* (2), 305–328.

Carrigan, Richard P. (2009). Implementing language acquisition in classrooms. *Education Digest, 75* (4), 57–61.

Cho, Seonhee, & Reich, Gabriel A. (2008). New immigrants, new challenges: High school social studies teachers and English language learner instruction. *The Social Studies, 99* (6), 235–242.

Christie, Kathy. (2008). Dat's story: Things have got to change. *Phi Delta Kappan, 89* (7), 469–470.

Chun, Christian W. (2009). Critical literacies and graphic novels for English-language learners: Teaching "Maus." *Journal of Adolescent & Adult Literacy, 53* (2), 144–153.

Coltrane, Bronwyn. (2002). *English language learners and high-stakes tests: An overview of the issues.* Retrieved from http://www.cal.org/resources/digest/0207coltrane.html

Derwing, Tracey M., DeCorby, Emilie, Ichikawa, Julia, & Jamieson, Kama. (1999). *Canadian Modern Language Review, 55* (4), 532–547.

Geinosky, Stephen, (2007). *Education takes new direction: Monmouth-Roseville adapting to rise in ESL students.* Retrieved from http://www.register-mail.com/stories/102807/MAI_BEM6GQDF.GID.shtml

Hu, Winnie. (2007, October 9). In some schools, iPods are required listening. *New York Times*, p. 1, Op.

Klein, Anna Maria. (2008). Sensitivity to the learning needs of newcomers in foreign language settings. *Multicultural Education, 16* (2), 41–44.

O'Loughlin, Judith, & Haynes, Judie. (2004). Organizing and assessing in the content area class. Retrieved from http://www.everythingesl.net/inservices/judith2.php

Payan, Rose M., & Nettles, Michael T. (n.d.). *Current state of English-language learners in the U.S. K–12 student population.* Retrieved from http://www.ets.org/Media/Conferences_and_Events/pdf/ELLsympsium/ELL_factsheet.pdf

Perkins-Gough, Deborah. (2007). Focus on adolescent English language learners. *Educational Leadership, 64* (6), 90–91.

Rance-Roney, Judith. (2009). Best practices for adolescent ELLS. *Educational Leadership, 66* (7), 32–37.

Short, Deborah J., & Fitzsimmons, Shannon. (2007). *Double the work: Challenges and solutions to acquiring language and academic literacy for adolescent English language learners—A report to the Carnegie Corporation of New York.* Washington, DC: Alliance for Excellent Education.

TESOL. (2006). *Position statement on adolescent English language learners in adult ESL programs in the United States.* Retrieved from http://www.tesol.org/s_tesol/bin.asp?CID=32&DID=5888&DOC=FILE.PDF

WIDA Consortium. (2007). *English Language Proficiency (ELP) Standards.* Retrieved from http://www.wida.us/standards/elp.aspx

Zehr, Mary Ann. (2007). Instructional model may yield gains for English-learners. *Education Week, 27* (14), 12.

Suggested Activities

1. Interview some recent immigrant adolescent English language learners. Ask them questions related to the challenges they face when enrolling in U.S. high schools.

2. Visit an inclusive high school classroom that has adolescent ELLs in attendance. Observe the ELLs and write a report comparing the behaviors of the ELLs and their English-speaking peers.

3. Locate research relating to the education of adolescent English language learners. Write a paper sharing key research findings.

4. Attend a meeting of school librarians and ask them how they serve the needs of the ELLs in their schools.

Learning More about Subject Areas

There are, of course, many more subject areas and programs in a school curriculum than the three discussed in this section. These chapters were intended to be representative and to serve as a guide for investigating other areas of the curriculum. The following is a list of subjects, programs, or support areas that can be researched at any of the appropriate levels—elementary, middle or high school.

- Advanced Placement or International Baccalaureate Courses
- Art
- Business
- Career Development and Occupational Studies
- English as a Second Language
- Family and Consumer Sciences
- Foreign Languages
- Guidance and Counseling
- Humanities
- Language Arts
- Math
- Music
- Physical Education
- Preschool Programs
- Reading
- Science
- Social Studies
- Technology Education

A quick way to determine what is being taught in classrooms is to interview or informally talk with teachers. This can also be accomplished by attending departmental meetings. In order to successfully collaborate with teachers it is helpful to have copies of textbooks and other major classroom resources in a professional library. Perusing the textbooks in a particular subject area will provide a good understanding of the content of the course. Creating curriculum maps of the media center collection and comparing the maps to the curriculum that is being taught is also an invaluable tool for relevant collection development.

In some high schools there may also be curriculum guides that provide detailed information about specific courses. Larger schools may have curriculum coordinators, and some school districts have coordinators of specific areas of the curriculum. These persons will have the most up-to-date information on subject standards, methods of assessment, and instructional methods. They most likely will also have a large collection of professional materials in specific subject areas.

Another means of educating one's self about subject areas is to obtain the names of the major national and state associations of the educators who teach in that area. Any teacher should be able to provide this information. Most of these organizations have extensive Web pages, including a discussion of standards, available resource materials, information about the professional journals they publish, conference information, and links to other Web pages that relate to the subject area. The best means of finding out the major issues and trends is to read articles in professional journals. Attending a conference in a particular subject area of the curriculum will also provide similar information.

Special Groups of Students and the School Librarian

Since the 1970s, students with special needs have been receiving more attention in both public and private education. This emphasis parallels the arousal of public sensitivity to persons who have disabilities, impairments, or other conditions that set them apart from the general population, as well as coinciding with the legislative actions the U.S. government and states have passed to deal with the needs of these persons.

Three groups of special students are discussed in the following chapters—autistic, highly mobile students, and students with gay, lesbian, bisexual, or transgender orientations. Concerns about how to address the needs of these students in schools have been just as intense as discussions about mainstreaming students with physical or learning disabilities.

In the following three chapters these concerns are addressed, and definitions and characteristics of the students are provided. Students with autism are part of a wide spectrum, from very low-functioning young people whose needs are usually addressed in special schools or classrooms to high-functioning students, such as those with Asperger's syndrome. Highly mobile students include a diverse group of students—children of migrant workers, students whose families are homeless, young people living in foster families, children of parents going through a divorce, immigrant young people, and the children of military families. Meeting the needs of lesbian, gay, bisexual, and transgender students in schools has probably caused the most controversy in recent years. The chapters also include discussion of any legislation that deals with these special groups of students, as well as the organizations and publications dedicated to the special groups.

One of the paramount values of librarianship is equitable access to information. Thus, being able to understand and address the needs of special groups of students is essential. School librarians must work cooperatively with teachers, administrators, and parents to see that all students in a school are provided access to the rich opportunities and materials that are available in school libraries.

CHAPTER **5**

Students Who Are Autistic

There has been much concern in recent years relating to the causes and apparent dramatic increase of the prevalence of autism spectrum disorder (ASD) in the United States and in some other countries. In February 2007 the Center for Disease Control and Prevention reported that autism had risen to 1 in every 150 children in the United States and almost 1 in every 94 boys (Autism Society, 2008). This is more than double the number of children diagnosed in 1996 (Becker, 2009).

Autism is a spectrum disease that is defined by a certain set of behaviors, but persons with autism can exhibit different combinations of the behaviors at various degrees of severity. Thus, every person with autism is an individual with a unique personality and combination of characteristics. The Autism Society (2008) lists some of the following traits that are exhibited by children with autism:

- Little or no eye contact with other people
- Lack of delay in spoken language
- Lack of spontaneous play
- Repetitive use of language or movements
- Lack of interest in relationships with peers
- Persistent fixation on parts of objects

Some children with autism are completely nonverbal, while others on the high end of the spectrum, such as those with Asperger's syndrome (AS), may be very talkative (Abramson, 2007).

The definition of autism was broadened in 1987 by the Diagnostic and Statistical Manual of Mental Disorders (DSM), and the disability evolved into a spectrum of disorders ranging from profound impairment to very mild challenges (Becker, 2009). Asperger's syndrome, which was originally defined 60 years ago, only recently became an accepted diagnosis on the autism spectrum (Stillman, 2004). Some clinicians refer to AS as "high functioning" autism. While the fourth edition of DSM grouped Asperger's syndrome under the umbrella heading *pervasive developmental disorders*, the fifth edition to be published in 2013 might fold AS into the autism category. This change of category could make it possible for children with AS to more easily receive assistance. Children with Asperger's syndrome differ from other children with autism because they do not display clinically significant delays in language, cognitive development, age-appropriate self-help skills, adaptive behaviors (other than social interaction), and curiosity about the environment (Stillman, 2004).

No one knows exactly what causes autism or why it impacts more boys than girls, but scientists are trying to discover if there is a chromosome or cluster of genes associated with it. However, a family that has a biologically related relative with autism is more likely to have a child with ASD than a family without such a relative (New England Center for Children, n.d.). Autism is believed to be a lifetime disorder with progress often very gradual (Whelan, 2009).

Legislation

In 1975 the U.S. Congress enacted Public Law 94–142, initially known as the Education for All Handicapped Children Law. In 2004 this federal act was reauthorized and is known as the Individuals with Disabilities Education Improvement Act of 2004 (P.L. 108–446) or IDEA. IDEA guarantees a free and appropriate public education for every child with learning disabilities, including children with autism. IDEA has both statutes and regulations, with the statutes as the language of the law, and the regulations as an explanation of how the law should be enacted (Autism Society, 2008).

The U.S. Congressional No Child Left Behind Act of 2001 (P.L. 107–110), commonly known as NCLB, also has applications to students with autism. The act was designed to provide a high-quality education to all students. It creates state-by-state accountability systems, and requires that the academic progress of underserved student population groups, including students with disabilities, be measured and reported.

Two other laws govern the educational rights of students with disabilities. The Family Educational Rights and Privacy Act (FERPA) protects the privacy of students' educational records, while Section 504 of the Rehabilitation Act protects the civil rights of persons with disabilities and prohibits discrimination against a person with a disability by any agency receiving federal funds. These laws are also important in understanding the rights of children with autism in public schools in the United States (Autism Society, 2008).

Educational Programming

Services and programs for students with autism vary from school district to school district and region to region. There are a variety of therapeutic and educational programs that are utilized with students with autism (Rudy, 2009).

Individualized Education Plans
Since each child with autism is unique, a good educational program for a child with autism really depends upon the needs of the child. To make certain that a child's educational needs

are met by a school district, the district follows IDEA, the federal law that guarantees that the child with a disability is entitled to a Free and Appropriate Education (FAPE). In a school, a team of educators and other persons with special expertise or knowledge about the child meet with parents of a child with a disability to develop an individualized education plan (IEP) that details in writing an approach to meet the unique needs of the child. The team sets goals that are specific to the child's needs and strengths. A method and a schedule for each goal should be included. There is also a statement in the document that should reflect why the child's educational placement is as inclusive as possible (called "least restrictive environment") as opposed to some other alternative placement (Stillman, 2004).

Inclusion

In the United States, schools must first consider the option of inclusion in a regular classroom for children with a disability. Inclusion refers to placing a child in a regular classroom and bringing the needed extra services to the children with special needs who are in the classroom. Inclusion works best for children who are high functioning on the autism spectrum and who are at least somewhat social; it is more challenging for children who are nonverbal (Rudy, 2009). According to Abramson (2007) schools are managing to work with children with ASD in inclusive classrooms. Historically, many school systems chose to educate these children in private schools. However, private schools are expensive so many school districts are currently trying to educate children with autism themselves. In California it is estimated that the average cost per pupil with autism is $36,000 in its public school systems (Asimov, 2008). This includes special services provided to the students. Private centers, such as the May Institute, a Boston-area research and education center for children with serious developmental delays, are expensive, with an average per year cost of $75,000 for day students (Abramson, 2007).

Some school districts have schools that serve as centers for students with autism. A self-contained classroom at such a center is headed by special education teachers who provide intensive intervention for students who are on the lower end of the autism spectrum. However, the goal is generally to move students to regular classrooms as soon as it is appropriate. Other options include having a resource special education classroom in a school where students can go for academic, social, or behavior support several times a day to take breaks from the regular classrooms. And still another option sometimes used in regular classrooms is to have paraprofessionals, who are trained to support the needs of any special education students, assist the regular classroom teachers. In any type of accommodation for students with disabilities it is important to have the regular classroom teacher and special education teacher work collaboratively to plan and implement the educational plans (IEPs) for students with special needs, including those with autism.

Organizations and Publications

The Autism Society of America and Autism Speaks are two of the most well-known organizations that provide information, resources, and support for parents and teachers of autism, as well as for persons with ASD. The Web site *Autism Resources*, www.autism-resources.com/links/organizations.html, lists autism-related organizations throughout the world. In the beginning of 2010, 77 organizations were listed for the United States, 14 for Canada, 10 for the United Kingdom, and several in other countries.

Jessica Kingsley Publishers, with addresses in London and Philadelphia, and Future Horizons, Inc., in Arlington, Texas, are the two leading publishers of resources dealing with autism and Asperger's syndrome. They both list over 100 resources available on the topics. In addition, Magination Press, an imprint of the American Psychological Association, publishes self-help books for children and for the adults in their lives. Their Web site includes books, videos, and articles on autism spectrum disorders. Autism Asperger Publishing Company, an independent publisher specializing in books on ASD, was established in 1999; their books target parents and professionals. Woodbine House Publishers is run by nine colleagues who work to publish books on various special needs, including autism. Their Web site lists numerous books about autism, including a few books that are available only online.

The Role of the School Librarian

The school librarian can work closely with teachers, as well as parents, to meet the needs of students with autism. It is essential for the school librarian to be aware of any students with special needs who are using the school library. School librarians who view the IEPs for such students can assist in the educational programming for students with special needs.

Students with ASD often have sensory sensitivities, with the most common sensitivities being auditory (including intolerable noise or frequency levels), smell, taste, visual, and touch (Stillman, 2004). Knowing this, school librarians can try to keep noise levels low when students with autism are present in a class that is visiting the library. Children with autism may react to loud noises by covering their ears with their hands. Students with ASD may not like to be touched by other students or by adults. Additionally, these students often will not maintain eye contact so school librarians need to realize this is not a lack of respect when talking with students with ASD. Fluorescent lighting bothers some children with autism so it is wise to use other types of lighting in libraries when possible.

Instructional Strategies

The same types of instructional strategies used by special education teachers or regular teachers, with mainstreamed students, can be used by the school librarian. Most children with ASD prefer predictable routines and settings. The school librarian can work with the regular classroom teacher by providing a photo of the school librarian that can be shared with students with ASD before the students' first visit to the school library. Also, since students with autism tend to be visual learners, a visual representation of the routine followed in the school library can be given to students with ASD and can also be placed on a poster in the school library. Such a representation might include lining up to walk to the school library from the classroom, entering the school library and sitting in the section where stories are read aloud, transitioning to tables after the stories are shared, working on a craft activity at the table, leaving a table to look for books in the shelf areas, taking books to the check-out desk, and finally lining up with the class at the end of the time in the school library. Line drawings or simple photos of these activities will help the students with ASD to understand and be comfortable with the routines that are followed in the school library. Children with ASD do not like surprises, even if they are good ones. According to Brenda Smith Myles, chief of programs for the Autism Society of American, "It totally throws them off because they do not know what to do" (Whelan, 2009, p. 33).

Some children with ASD will not ask for help so frequent intervention, such as checking to see they have been able to find the books that they want, can be handled by the school librarian or library clerk. Whelan (2009) also recommends keeping language simple and concrete and avoiding idioms or jokes. Students with ASD tend to be very literal minded. If you ask a student with ASD if they are "ready to roll," they may respond by rolling on the floor (Crisman, 2008). It should be remembered, however, that these students like to laugh just like any other children; they just need to understand the humor.

Assigning a peer buddy to a child with ASD will not only help with social interaction, but will also help the child be more comfortable in the library setting. Such buddies, however, should receive some training from a parent or special education teacher. Using student volunteers as buddies will also help dispel the fears and conceptions of other children about this disability (Whelan, 2009).

Modifying library assignments to fit the needs of students with ASD is another instructional strategy that can be used successfully by the school librarian. If regular students are asked to complete 10 items in a library scavenger hunt, the activity sheet given to students with autism might ask for only five items and could include some visual picture representations of the types of items that the students are asked to locate.

Some modifications in the story times may also need to be made. For instance, students with autism may need to sit on a carpet square so they understand the boundaries or they may need a copy of the book that is being read or they may want to hold a stuffed animal for comfort (Whelan, 2009). These students might display repetitive behaviors that they have difficulty controlling, such as rocking back and forth, pacing, or wiggling. If the behaviors are not bothering other students, it is best to ignore the behaviors. However, intervention is needed for screaming, meltdowns, destructive behavior, inappropriate sexual behavior, or instances where a student is going to hurt himself or others (Scotch Plains Public Library & Fanwood Memorial Library, 2008).

Because technology uses a variety of formats, often has many images, accepts nonverbal responses, and does not usually require high social skills it can significantly help students with autism (Farmer & Sykes, 2008). Some students with ASD have difficulty with fine motor skills so using a computer, rather than writing with a pencil or pen, can be beneficial. Some older students with Asperger's syndrome seem to have a natural ability to understand computer languages and are skilled at computer programming and creating computer graphics (Attwood, 2008).

Helpful Resources
Teacher and Parent Resource Collections
In recent years there have been many resources about autism produced by publishers for teachers and parents. Parents and educators look to books and other information formats for help and hope in dealing with disabilities. One of the most valuable services that the school librarian can provide teachers and parents is how to locate and evaluate these resources, including the Web sites that provide information about autism. There are many resources dealing with ASD that can be included in a collection for teachers and parents.

The following titles are some that school librarians should definitely consider providing in such collections.

Attwood, Tony. (2008). *The complete guide to Asperger's syndrome.* London: Jessica Kingsley Publishers.

This book is considered essential reading for families, teachers, and other professionals who deal with persons with Asperger's syndrome, as well as for persons with Asperger's syndrome. It draws on the experiences and cases that Attwood, a clinical psychologist in Australia, has encountered with his clients. The book has been translated into 20 different languages. Attwood has written several other books and papers that deal with Asperger's syndrome and is widely recognized as an expert on the topic.

Fine, Deborah, & Dunn, Michelle. (2007). *Autism in your classroom.* Bethesda, MD: Woodbine House Publishers.

Written by neuropsychologists with extensive clinical and classroom experiences, this book is an easy-to-read guide for elementary school teachers. Included in the book are an overview of ASD, a variety of strategies to manage the learning and behavior of students with autism, and two useful cases studies.

Moor, Julia. (2008). *Playing, laughing, and learning with children on the autism spectrum* (2nd ed.). London: Jessica Kingsley Publishers.

Users of the book have highly recommended this practical guide for parents that provides numerous suggestions on how to involve children with autism in interactive play. This second edition of the book also contains information about how to use computers and the Internet with children with ASD.

Notbohm, Ellen. (2006). *Ten things your student with autism wishes you knew.* Arlington, TX: Future Horizons.

Educators will benefit from Notbohm's concise and practical book that deals with how to work with students with autism in the classroom. The author helps educators understand the thinking patterns of students with ASD and provides suggestions on how to encourage the students to progress and achieve.

Scotch Plains Public Library & Fanwood Memorial Library. (2008). *Libraries and autism: We're connected.* Scotch Plains, NJ & Fanwood, NJ: Fanwood Memorial Library.

This award-winning video was produced by two New Jersey public libraries as a customer-service training video for library staffers. It has received national and international attention in the library and autism communities. The video can be accessed at http://www.thejointlibrary.org/autism/video.htm and is also present on YouTube.

Stillman, William. (2004). *The everything parent's guide to children with Asperger's syndrome: Help, hope, and guidance.* Avon, MA: Adams Media.

This is another must-read book for parents of children who have been diagnosed with Asperger's syndrome. The author presents advice on how to deal with problems that might occur from early childhood through college. Clear examples in straightforward language are presented.

Books for Students

There are many books on the market that are written to inform typical students about peers with autism, as this seems to be a growing genre. Also, more books for young people that include characters with ASD are being published each year. A few of those that have received good reviews from professional journals, organizations dedicated to autism, or users of the books are listed below. School librarians will not have difficulty finding other similar types of books to add to their collections.

Amento, Charles A., III. (1992). *Russell is extra special: A book about autism for children.* Washington, DC: Magination Press.
    Although it may seem dated because of its publication date, this book remains popular in schools and libraries. The author, a physician, wrote the book about his son who has ASD. The clear language makes it easy for children to understand.

Baskin, Nora Raleigh. (2009). *Anything but typical.* New York: Simon & Schuster.
    Sixth-grader Jason, who has ASD, is not able to communicate freely with others in person, but he finds his voice through writing stories on the computer. This fictionalized account of a young boy struggling with the challenges of ASD is recommended for students 9–12 years of age.

Bishop, Beverly. (2003). *My friend with autism: A coloring book for peers and siblings.* Arlington, TX: Future Horizons.
    The author who is a parent of a child with ASD wrote this book for students in her son's elementary school. It is written for children who are 9–12 years of age, but can be used successfully for younger students.

Elder, Jennifer. (2005). *Different like me: My book of autism heroes.* London: Jessica Kingsley.
    This book intended for children ages 8–12 is written in child-friendly language. It includes the lives of various famous people from science, art, math, philosophy, and comedy who had ASD and found it difficult to fit into society.

Erskine, Kathryn. (2010). *Mockingbird.* New York: Philomel.
    Fifth-grader Caitlin, who was diagnosed with Asperger's syndrome, must deal with the tragic death of her older brother in a middle school shooting. This moving story, which draws somewhat on the theme of Harper Lee's *To Kill a Mockingbird*, has had rave reviews. The book is recommended for young people 10 years of age and older.

Ginsberg, Blaze. (2009). *Episodes: My life as I see it.* New York: Roaring Brook.
    Ginsberg's fascinating memoirs of his world is presented to readers in an unusual format inspired by the Web site IMDb.com. Ginsberg, a high-functioning young person with AS, gives readers a glimpse of an adolescent mind that is wired differently. The book has received excellent reviews and is available in audio and MP3 formats.

Hoopman, Kathy. (2006). *All cats have Asperger's syndrome.* London: Jessica Kingsley.
    This delightful book compares the characteristics of children with Asperger's syndrome to characteristics of cats. The accompanying illustrations help children

understand how they are different from their peers and highlights the unique qualities of individuals with AS.

Isaacson, Rupert. (2009). *The horse boy: A father's quest to heal his son.* Boston: Little, Brown.
This fascinating, true story relates the journey of the author, his wife, and five-year-old son Rowan to Mongolia. There they consult with the shamans and original horse people to help them heal Rowan, who had been diagnosed with autism but seemed to improve by riding horses. The book is available in audio format, and an award-winning documentary movie based on the book opened in theaters in 2009.

Larson, Elaine Marie. (2006). *I am utterly unique: Celebrating the strengths of children with Asperger syndrome and high functioning autism.* Shawnee Mission, KS: Autism Asperger Publishing.
The unique characteristics and abilities of children with AS are presented in an A to Z format. The book is designed to help children with AS grow in awareness of their abilities.

Lears, Laurie. (2003). *Ian's walk: A story about autism.* Park Ridge, IL: Albert Whitman.
This high-quality picture book will engage students from ages 6–10. The story about Julie, a young girl who loses her brother with ASD in the park, deals with the embarrassment that Julie feels about her brother's actions. Julie thinks like her brother in order to find him.

Lord, Cynthia. (2006). *Rules.* New York: Scholastic.
This humorous award-winning novel (Newbery Honor Book and Schneider Family Book Award winner) is told from the viewpoint of 12-year-old Catherine, whose brother David has autism. The book is recommended for 9 to 12 year-olds and is a great book for siblings of children with ASD.

Shally, Celeste. (2006). *Since we're friends: An autism picture book.* New York: Watering Can Press.
Told from the point of view of a typical student, this book describes a variety of scenarios in which autistic children might have problems. The book, which is intended for ages 9–12, helps children understand people who are different from them and the challenges that people with autism might face.

Shapiro, Ouisie. (2009). *Autism and me: Sibling stories.* Park Ridge, IL: Albert Whitman.
With colorful photos by Steven Vote, this book tells the first-person stories of siblings of children with autism. The struggles and challenges of living with a sibling with autism are presented through interviews.

Stork, Francisco X. (2009). *Marcelo in the real world.* New York: Arthur Levine/Scholastic.
Seventeen-year-old Marcelo, a teen with Asperger's syndrome who attends a special school for young people with disabilities, is pushed by his father to work during the summer in his father's law firm so Marcelo can experience the real world. This coming-of-age novel for YAs has been placed on several best books lists.

Velasco, Joanna Keating. (2007). *A is for autism F is for friend*. Shawnee Mission, KS: Autism Asperger Publishing.

The author takes us through the day of Chelsea, a young girl with severe autism. The book is a good tool for educating students about autism and can be used in a discussion-oriented format.

Conclusions

The number of students being diagnosed with autism has more than doubled since 1996 and does not seem to be slowing down. These children vary from those with severe disabilities to students with high-functioning disabilities, such as Asperger's syndrome. Most school districts are currently placing many of these students in mainstream or inclusive classroom settings, where their special services are being brought to the classroom. School librarians are helping meet the needs of students with autism by providing specialized resources for students, as well as for parents and teachers of children with autism. Librarians are also learning and implementing instructional strategies that work well for students with autism.

References

Abramson, Larry. (2007). *Public schools prepare to educate kids with autism*. Retrieved from http://www.npr.org/templates/story/story.php?storyId=12776434

Asimov, Nanette. (2008). *State's schools lack cohesive plan for autism*. Retrieved from http://articles.sfgate.com/2008-07-13/bay-area/17173413_1_autism-spectrum-disorders-disabled-child-education-s-autism-advisory-committee/2

Attwood, Tony. (2008). *The complete guide to Asperger's syndrome*. London: Jessica Kingsley Publishers.

Autism Society. (2008). *About autism*. Retrieved from http://www.autism-society.org

Becker, Jody. (2009). *Behind the autism statistics*. Retrieved from http://www.theatlantic.com/doc/200910u/autism-diagnoses

Crisman, Belinda W. (2008). Inclusive programming for students with autism. *Principal, 88* (2), 28–32.

Farmer, Lesley S. J., & Syles, Maureen. (2008). Library services for students with autism. *CSLA Journal, 31* (2), 25–27.

New England Center for Children. (n.d.). *Autism resources*. Retrieved from http://www.necc.org/autism_resources/fact_sheets.asp

Rudy, Lisa Jo. (2009). *Educational options for children with autism*. Retrieved from http://autism.about.com/od/schoolandsummer/a/edoptionshub.htm

Scotch Plains Public Library & Fanwood Memorial Library. (2008). *Libraries and autism: We're connected* [DVD]. Scotch Plains, NJ & Fanwood, NJ: Fanwood Memorial Library.

Stillman, William. (2004). *The everything parent's guide to children with Asperger's syndrome: Help, hope, and guidance*. Avon, MA: Adams Media.

Whelan, Debra Lau. (2009). The equal opportunity disorder. *School Library Journal, 55* (8), 30–34.

Suggested Activities

1. Prepare a list of questions and interview one or more parents of children with autism. Share what you learned either in an oral or print format.

2. Get permission from a school and parent where students with autism are mainstreamed into regular classrooms. Then observe a student with autism who is in an inclusive or mainstream classroom. Share which characteristics discussed in the chapter were demonstrated by the student.

3. Observe the instructional strategies that are used by teachers and paraprofessionals in an inclusive classroom that contains one or more students with autism.

4. Interview a school librarian in a school where students with autism use the school library. Ask the school librarian what challenges are presented by having the students in the school library and how the librarian tries to meet the needs of the students.

CHAPTER 6

Highly Mobile Students

The United States has one of the highest national mobility rates, with about one-fifth of the population moving each year. It has become increasingly uncommon for students to attend schools in the same district or state during their education from kindergarten through high school (Titus, 2007). Families move for a variety of reasons, including divorce or family separation, home foreclosures, natural disasters, and job changes. Children of migrant workers move from state to state, following crop harvests. Students who are placed in foster care often change schools, and immigrants enroll in new schools as they enter the United States. Children of military personnel, missionaries, diplomats, and executives of international companies are mobile, not only in the United States, but on a global scale.

Poor and minority students, children of farmworkers, immigrants, the homeless, and foster children are particularly prone to high mobility rates. As more and more families face foreclosures on their homes or lose their jobs, the number of homeless students is increasing.

Legislation

A primary piece of legislation dealing with highly mobile students is the McKinney-Vento Act (P.L. 100–77), which was first signed by President Ronald Reagan in 1987. The McKinney Act originally consisted of 15 programs providing a range of services to homeless people. It has been amended several times and governs the education of children and youth in homeless situations. The law ensures that homeless children have transportation to school, and parents may choose the school that their children attend. It also ensures immediate enrollment of students, regardless of unpaid fines at current or previous schools. The National Association for the Education of Homeless Children and Youth (NAEHCY) and the National Law Center on Homelessness and Poverty collaborated to produce a document that answers frequently asked questions about the education rights of homeless children and youth. That document can be accessed at http://www.naehcy.org/faq.html. In order to implement the act, states must designate a statewide homeless coordinator to review policies and procedures. Some states have done well in complying with the act, while others have failed and are experiencing law suits because of their noncompliance.

Another federal law that applies to many highly mobile students is Title I of the No Child Left Behind Act of 2001 (NCLB). This title was a reauthorization of the Elementary and Secondary Education Act (ESEA) of 1965 that was part of President Lyndon B. Johnson's War on Poverty. The purpose of Title I of NCLB is to ensure that all children have fair and equal opportunity to obtain high-quality education. To meet the educational needs of students living in poverty, states receive federal funds; state educational agencies (SEAs) must make decisions on how to allocate the funds. Local educational agencies (LEAs) also have guidelines to determine the use of Title I funds. Accountability of performance on state standardized achievement tests is also a part of Title I, and schools, SEAs, and LEAs must report disaggregated achievement data for the following groups of students: high poverty, minority race/ethnicity, limited English proficiency, and disabilities. NCLB provides additional requirements and consequences when adequate yearly progress (APY) is not made (Popp, Stronge, & Hindman, 2003). More information about Title I and NCLB can be obtained by visiting the U.S. Department of Education Web site: http://www2.ed.gov/nclb/landing.jhtml.

Another part of Title I of NCLB deals specifically with children of migrant workers. The Migrant Education Program (MEP) is funded through Part C of Title I and is intended to ensure high-quality education services for migratory children by preventing these students from being penalized for lacking continuity and alignment for curriculum, academic status, and graduation requirements that vary from state to state. Funding is allocated to states based on previous counts of migratory children living in states (Popp, Stronge, & Hindman, 2003). More information about MEP can be found by accessing the U.S. Department of Education Web site: http://www2.ed.gov/programs/mep/index.html.

As mandated by the U.S. Congress in Section 1308 of the Elementary and Secondary Education Act and amended by NCLB of 2001, the U.S. Department of Education assists states in developing effective methods for electronic transfer of records. The Migrant Student Information Exchange (MSIX) is the technology that was developed by the Department of Education to allow states to share educational and health information on migrant children. This helps fulfill the department's mission to ensure appropriate enrollment, placement, and accrual of credits for migrant children nationwide. MSIX is operational, and the Department of Education is working with each state to implement MSIX. More information about record transfer of migrant youth can be found at the following U.S Department of Education Web site: www2.ed.gov/admins/lead/account/recordstransfer.html.

Impact of Student Mobility

When mobility of students becomes excessive and classrooms become a revolving door this can severely undermine a school's ability to show the benefits of touted educational reforms, such as smaller classes, improved facilities, and better-trained teachers (Hartman, 2006). Frequent school changes also negatively impact students. Research suggests that high student mobility affects students academically, psychologically, and socially (Rumberger, 2002). Students who make frequent school changes experience disruption in their home life, a lack of continuity in the content of their academic lessons, loss of friends, and often feelings of alienation.

Highly mobile students often face numerous challenges that can affect their success in school. Several research studies have indicated that students who change schools frequently are lower achievers than nonmobile students (Engec, 2006). Students who move frequently also have a lower school attendance rate and are twice as likely to repeat a grade (Popp, Stronge, & Hindman, 2003). Rumberger (2003) also noted that mobility during high school reduces students' prospects of graduating. These detrimental impacts of high mobility can also harm stable students by slowing down the pace of the curriculum and creating emotional disturbances stemming from sudden disappearances of classmates and friends (Hartman, 2006).

School districts are impacted negatively because of the high fiscal and administrative costs associated with high-need, highly mobile students. Transfer records of outgoing students need to be sent; health records of new students need to be procured; and other requirements of dealing with transient students can influence decisions relating to staff needs and use of resources. Additionally, school district administrators express strong concern that school testing assessments have been negatively affected by having highly mobile students in their schools (Pennsylvania State College of Education, 2010).

Lack of prompt transfer of school records can cause both administrative and pedagogical problems. Students without complete records may be given inappropriate placement while their school awaits their records for several weeks or even months. The use of electronically based record systems in some states has helped somewhat to alleviate this problem.

In the past, another challenge for schools was whether schools were required to verify legal immigration. However, in 1982 the U.S. Supreme Court ruled in *Plyler v. Doe* that schools have no legal obligation or authority to enforce U.S. immigration laws. Thus, undocumented children have the same rights as U.S. citizens to attend public schools (Popp, Stronge, & Hindman, 2003). Many of the children enrolling in schools not only do not speak English, but moreover may be illiterate in their own languages. The education of the parents of such children may be limited, and the parents may not be able to help their children with academic tasks. Furthermore, they may also lack the necessary resources to assist their children with homework assignments.

Despite the fact that most parents of migrant children work full-time, three-fifths of these children live in poverty, which leads to inadequate health care and frequent school absences (Walls, 2003). Migratory children also have linguistic and cultural differences that tend to isolate them from their peers. A report published by the U.S. Department of Education (2002) found that schools with large percentages of migrant children had lower expectations of student performance, less consistent standards and assessments, and fewer experienced teachers than other schools. The Migrant Education Program (MEP) was developed by the federal government to address these problems.

As the economy worsens and job losses increase, school officials are seeing many homeless families, including those from middle-class backgrounds. In 2009 it was predicted that two million children would lose their homes because of the foreclosure crisis (McKibben, 2009). Families who are homeless may be reluctant to share information of their condition because of the stigma that can be associated with homelessness. Thus, it is difficult for administrators to obtain accurate numerical counts of the homeless youth attending their schools. Research studies have indicated that more than half of homeless students do not attend school on a regular basis (Popp, Stronge, & Hindman, 2003).

While more prevalent in urban settings, homeless students can also be found in rural and suburban communities. Lack of services in rural areas adds an additional challenge to serve the needs of rural homeless students.

All homeless families are generally experiencing high levels of stress, and the children in these families have a strong need for stability. The McKinney-Vento Act helps deal with the stability concerns by requiring schools to immediately enroll children, even without records, and also by allowing students to remain in the school of their choice, even if the shelter where they live is not in that school district. The act also requires that every school district have a local homeless education liaison to build awareness of the needs of homeless students in the community and in the school system.

Children in foster care are one of the most educationally vulnerable student populations, with an estimated 542,000 children in the United States in foster care (Zetlin & Weinberg, 2004). The majority of these students come from backgrounds of poverty, and they are more likely than other children to have academic and behavioral trouble in school. They have high rates of absenteeism, and while 10 percent of the general population receives special education services, 25 percent to 52 percent of children in foster care are placed in special education (Zetlin & Weinberg, 2004). Data collected in California revealed that children in foster care attend an average of nine different schools by the time they are 18 years old (Kelly, 2000). With transfer of student records often delayed, teachers and administrators do not know how to serve the needs of foster children. Often this results in a child's active individualized education plan (IEP) not being implemented until new schools can do their own assessments.

All branches of the U.S. military employ persons whose children experience numerous moves because of the career choice of their parents. Thirty-five percent of children in military families change schools each year (Popp, Stronge, & Hindman, 2003). Not only do these children change schools frequently, but their parents also share some of the other characteristics of highly mobile families, with 32 percent to 50 percent of the families qualifying for free or reduced lunches (poverty indications) for their children and 94 percent of the parents having no more education than a high school diploma. Yet studies indicate that Department of Defense Schools (DoDS) consistently document student achievement equal to or surpassing those of students attending public schools.

Children gain their self-awareness through the connections they make with others, as well as their connections with places and possessions. When they move frequently these connections are lessened or sometimes totally disappear. The stress that highly mobile students experience can lead to a loss of identity and in some cases depression. In her interviews with highly mobile students, Rhodes (2008) noted that when students face a school change, many experience fear, loneliness, embarrassment, and anxiety. The mobile students stated that they were unable to focus on academic concerns until they could secure a peer group with whom they could interact. Finding how to reinforce self-awareness and lessen stressors for highly mobile students is a challenge for both schools and parents.

School Efforts

As evident from the previous discussion, the challenges of effectively dealing with highly mobile students in schools are numerous. Federal and state legislation have addressed some of the problems facing highly mobile families. Schools, however, can also do their part.

Highly mobile urban students discussed the impressions of their first day in a new school when interviewed by Rhodes (2008) and noted the importance of their first day. Schools can facilitate the acclimation of new students by providing structures for transitional services and community building. At their initial enrollment, students and their parents should be welcomed by a reception committee. A tour of the school needs to be provided, and parents should be given handbooks containing school policies and procedures. Parents should be informed of the importance of their involvement in the school and in the education of their children. Classroom buddies can be assigned for new students to help them begin the all-important socialization process.

Other steps that can be taken to facilitate the transition of new students into a school include:

- Improve the school's record keeping on student mobility.
- Send home forms in more than one language (Spanish for migrant children).
- Identify parent liaisons, including those who speak families' home languages, who can explain school programs to parents (Smith, Fien, & Paine, 2008).
- Make a concerted effort to learn a student's history.
- Identify a staff member who can check in with each student and family frequently during the first few weeks in the school (Smith, Fien, & Paine, 2008).
- Schedule a parent conference within a few weeks of a student's enrollment. If needed, have a translator available (Smith, Fien, & Paine, 2008).
- Hire school social workers and guidance counselors who are aware of the needs of highly mobile students.
- Provide school nurses to help care for health issues of highly mobile children who may not have primary care professionals.
- Educate teachers about foster care and its impact on foster care children.
- Provide ongoing professional development for teachers who deal with highly mobile students.
- Look for signs of homelessness—wearing same clothes every day, falling asleep in class, or hoarding food.
- Have clean clothes available for homeless and migrant children; organize a clothes collection for gently used clothing that can be used for students in need.
- Enhance students' self-concepts by helping them become a part of the group; avoid pull-out tutoring programs that separate them from classmates.
- As an alternative to pull-out programs during the day, provide after-school tutoring and mentoring (Zetlin & Weinberg, 2004).
- Teach social skills to any students who have such a need.
- Learn about the cultures of highly mobile students and integrate the knowledge of the cultures into the curriculum and student interactions.
- Use relevant cultural and ethnic literature in the curriculum (Romanski, 2003).
- Establish an attendance incentive program (Smith, Fien, & Paine, 2008).
- Monitor and support the students' needs throughout their stay in a school, not just in their initial enrollment.
- Make certain there is a yearlong focus on transition that includes school leaders, teachers, counselors, parents, family members, and the students themselves (Summers & Moehnke, 2006).
- Try to retain students if the reason for transfer is internal to the school district; offer transportation assistance if it would enable students to remain at their schools.

- Provide financial aid information and assistance in filling out applications for graduating students who hope to attend college.
- Prepare for students' departures to make them as efficient and stress-free as possible.

Newly homeless families may not know how to navigate social services, which thus prolongs the problems that their children have inside and outside school (McKibben, 2009). Therefore, it is important to inform homeless families of their rights and the services that their children are eligible to receive. School officials should assure homeless students they do not need to leave school even if they are temporarily in housing outside the school boundaries (McKibben, 2009). Parents should be provided information about public services that are available to their families (health insurance, child care, transportation, food, showers, counseling). Schools can coordinate with local liaisons for the homeless, as well as with shelter workers, to help inform homeless families about services available to them.

As mentioned previously, the educational achievements of highly mobile students in Department of Defense Schools do not seem to be impacted as seriously as those in the general population. The Department of Defense (DoD) has an excellent track record with regard to student mobility. It carries out timely transfer of records, maintains efficient record keeping, and has clearly specified course transfer agreements and graduation requirements. One particularly sensitive policy is to allow a family to remain at the duty assignment for an extra year if a student is entering or in the senior year of high school (Hartman, 2006).

The DoD schools use a Student to Student (S2S) transition program for high schools and a Junior Student to Student (JS2S) transition program for middle schools. These are research-based programs developed through a partnership between U.S. Army Child and Youth Services and the Military Child Education Coalition (MCEC). The programs are student-centered and student-led. They follow the "train the trainers" model so teams of students are responsible for training more students in each of their schools. New students are assisted in making immediate and positive peer contacts and thus are able to focus on academics immediately (Summers & Moehnke, 2006).

All the military branches have devised strategies to address the challenges of their highly mobile families. Strategies include establishing family and education support, encouragement of parental involvement, use of school counselors trained to meet the needs of military youth, and the development of a corporate culture that supports families and encourages school-family-military partnerships. Their programs also include high expectations for student and school success, as well as the expectation that parents participate in the child's education by attending parent meetings and volunteering in the schools (Walls, 2003). Public school officials could benefit by studying these strategies utilized by the U.S. military branches and adapting them to their schools.

The Role of the School Librarian

The school librarian can welcome highly mobile students and their families into the school by inviting them into the school library where they are able to receive an orientation to the library, with printed materials about procedures and library programs provided in both

English and in the first language of the families. This may necessitate finding other students in the school or persons in the community to help with translation.

Students should be assured that the school library is a safe and positive environment, where all students are welcome. Since other students may tend to tease or bully highly mobile students, it is important for the school librarian to be constantly aware of such behavior and take steps to prevent harmful treatment of other students. Both the discussion and modeling of respect for others should be evident in the school library.

Helpful Resources

As with any other special groups of students, highly mobile students need to see their lives and families represented in the materials that are available in the school library. Both fiction and nonfiction books that relate to highly mobile students should be included in the school library collection, and many can be shared in story times or displays. The following are some suggested titles:

Homeless

Berck, Judith. (1992). *No place to be: Voices of homeless children.* New York: Houghton Mifflin. Recommended for young adults.

Bunting, Eve. (1993). *Fly away home.* New York: Clarion. Recommended for ages 4–8.

Chalofsky, Margie, Wallace, Judy, & Finland, Glen. (1992). *Changing places: A kid's view of shelter living.* Mt. Rainier, MD: Gryphon House. Recommended for ages 9–12.

DiSalvo-Ryan, Dyanne. (1997). *Uncle Willie and the soup kitchen.* New York: William Morrow. Recommended for ages 4–8.

Groth, Bonnie Lee. (1995). *Home is where we live: Life at a shelter through a girl's eyes.* Chicago: Cornerstone Press. Recommended for ages 4–8.

Gunning, Monica. (2004). *A shelter in our car.* San Francisco: Children's Book Press. Recommended for ages 4–8.

Kozol, Jonathon. (2006). *Rachel and her children: Homeless families in America.* New York: Three Rivers Press. Recommended for young adults.

McGovern, Ann. (1999). *The lady in the box.* New York: Turtle Books. Recommended for ages 4–8.

Polacco, Patricia. (1999). *I can hear the sun: A modern myth.* New York: Putnam Juvenile. Recommended for ages 4–8.

Testa, Marie. (1996). *Someplace to go.* Park Ridge, IL: Albert Whitman. Recommended for ages 4–8.

Migrant and Immigrants

Atkins, S. Beth. (2000). *Voices from the fields: Children of migrant farmworkers tell their stories.* New York: Little Brown. Recommended for ages 9–12.

Bunting, Eve. (1997). *A day's work.* New York: Clarion Books. Recommended for ages 4–8.

Jimenez, Francisco. (2000). *La Mariposa.* New York: Houghton Mifflin. Recommended for ages 4–8.

Jimenez, Francisco. (2002). *Breaking through.* New York: Houghton Mifflin. Recommended for young adults.

Perez, L. King. (2002). *First day in grapes.* New York: Lee & Low. Recommended for ages 4–8.

Ryan, Pam Munoz. (2002). *Esperanza rising.* New York: Scholastic. Recommended for ages 9–12.

Suarez-Orozco, Carola. (2002). *Children of immigration.* Cambridge, MA: Harvard University Press. Recommended for young adults.

Suarez-Orozco, Carola, Suarez-Orozco, Marcelo M., & Todorova, Irina. (2008). *Learning a new land: Immigrant students in American society.* Cambridge, MA: Harvard University Press. Recommended for young adults.

Foster Children and Orphans

Creech, Sharon. (2002). *Ruby Holler.* New York: Harper Collins. Recommended for ages 9–12.

Dowell, Frances O'Roark. (2004). *Where I'd like to be.* New York: Atheneum. Recommended for young adults.

Gibbons, Kaye. (1997). *Ellen Foster.* New York: Vintage Books. Recommended for young adults.

Grimes, Nikki. (2006). *The road to Paris.* New York: Putnam Juvenile. Recommended for ages 9–12.

Hansen, Joyce. (2005). *One true friend.* New York: Clarion Books. Recommended for ages 9–12.

Hobbs, Will. (1999). *The maze.* New York: Harper Collins. Recommended for young adults.

Horvath, Polly. (2008). *Everything on a waffle.* New York: Farrar, Straus & Giroux. Recommended for ages 9–12.

Levy, Janice. (2004). *Finding the right spot: When kids can't live with their parents.* Washington, DC: Magination Press. Recommended for ages 4–8.

Nelson, Julie. (2006). *Families change: A book for children experiencing termination of parental rights.* Minneapolis: Free Spirit Publishing. Recommended for ages 4–8.

Pelzer, Dave. (1997). *The lost boy: A foster child's search for the love of a family.* Deerfield Beach, FL: Health Communications. Recommended for young adults.

Wilgocki, Jennifer, & Wright, Marcia Kahn. (2002). *Maybe days: A book for children in foster care.* Washington, DC: Magination Press. Recommended for ages 4–8.

Wilgocki, Jennifer, & Wright, Marcia Kahn. (2002). *The star: A story to help young children understand foster care.* Washington, DC: Magination Press. Recommended for ages 4–8.

Wolfson, Jill. (2006). *Home and other big fat lies.* New York: Henry Holt. Recommended for ages 9–12.

Military

Christiansen, Rebecca, & Armstrong, Jewel. (2007). *My dad's a hero.* Tarentum, PA: Word Association. Recommended for ages 4–8.

Cooney, Caroline. (1992). *Operation: Homefront.* New York: Laurel Leaf. Recommended for young adults.

Donahue, John. (2001). *Till tomorrow.* New York: Farrar, Straus & Giroux. Recommended for young adults.

Franklin, Kristine L. (2006). *Dove song.* Cambridge, MA: Candlewick Press. Recommended for young adults.

Gantos, Jack. (2005). *Jack adrift: Fourth grade without a clue.* New York: Farrar, Straus & Giroux. Recommended for ages 9–12.

Giff, Patricia Reilly. (1999). *Lily's crossing.* New York: Delacorte Press Books for Young Readers. Recommended for ages 9–12.

Mead, Alice. (2009). *Soldier mom.* New York: Farrar, Straus & Giroux. Recommended for ages 9–12.

Pelton, Mindy L. (2004). *When Dad's at sea.* Morton Grove, IL: Albert Whitman. Recommended for ages 6–9.

Spinelli, Eileen. (2008). *While you are away.* New York: Hyperion. Recommended for ages 4–8.

If books on one of the topics listed above are read during a story time, the school librarian should then lead a discussion about the story, concentrating on questions that deal with the challenges faced by highly mobile students. The school librarian can also ask students to share stories of what it is like to be in a new school or new place. Including books about highly mobile students in book talks is an additional way to share the book titles.

Collaborating with Others

There are numerous ways that the school librarian can work with others in the school or community to serve the needs of highly mobile students. Collaborating with teachers on relevant lessons or developing projects that deal with social justice is particularly important. School librarians can make certain that research materials are available on topics such as homelessness, poverty, migrant workers, and foster care.

Working with others in the school, the librarian can help sponsor after-school programs that provide tutoring and homework assistance for highly mobile students. The school librarian can also help organize a family resource center in the school. Such a center should include materials in multiple languages (Smith, Fien, & Paine, 2008).

Additionally school librarians can be active in the community by helping provide computer access in shelters or public libraries so homeless children have an opportunity to complete their homework assignments and their parents have access to information relating to social services that might be available to them and to their children. Supporting local events held in shelters or community centers by advertising them in the school is another way that the librarian can assist highly mobile students.

Conclusions

The prevalence of highly mobile students in public schools is on the increase. The needs of these students are great and although there has been some success with legislation to deal with the challenges of educating homeless, migrant, immigrant and foster care children, more effort should be put into solving the problems of effectively transitioning and educating these highly mobile students. School officials and educators could benefit by researching and modeling school programs, such as the Department of Defense Schools, that have done well in meeting the needs of highly mobile students. School librarians can make positive contributions to solving the problems of highly mobile students by providing relevant resources, welcoming highly mobile students and families into their libraries, and collaborating with school and community personnel to provide the needed services for the families and students.

References

Engec, Necati. (2006). The relationship between mobility and student performance and behavior. *The Journal of Educational Research, 99* (3), 167–178.

Hartman, Chester. (2006). Students on the move. *Educational Leadership, 63* (5), 20–24.

Kelly, Kathleen. (2000). The education crisis for children in the California Juvenile Court System. *Hastings Constitutional Law Quarterly, 27,* 757–773.

McKibben, Sarah. (2009). Foreclosed: Two million homeless students and counting. *Education Digest, 74* (9), 9–11.

Pennsylvania State College of Education. (2010). *Poverty, housing insecurity and student transiency in rural areas.* Retrieved from http://www.ed.psu.edu/educ/crec/research/poverty

Popp, Patricia A., Stronge, James H., & Hindman, Jennifer L. (2003). Students on the move: Reaching and teaching highly mobile children and youth. Greensboro, NC: National Center for Homeless Education at SERVE. (ERIC Document Reproduction Service, No. ED 482 661).

Rhodes, Virginia L. (2008). Learning on the go: Voices of highly mobile urban students. *Learning Inquiry, 2* (2), 113–125.

Romanowski, Michael H. (2003). Meeting the unique needs of the children of migrant workers. *Clearing House, 77* (1), 27–33.

Rumberger, Russell. (2002). Student mobility and academic achievement. ERIC Digest. Champaign, IL: ERIC Clearinghouse on Elementary and Early Childhood Education. (ERIC Document Reproduction Service No. ED 466 314).

Rumberger, Russell. (2003). The causes and consequences of student mobility. *Journal of Negro Education, 72* (1), 6–21.

Smith, Jean Louise M., Fien, Hank, & Paine, Stan C. (2008). When mobility disrupts learning. *Educational Leadership, 65* (7), 59–63.

Summers, Al, & Moehnke, Larry. (2006). Meeting the needs of students in transition. *Middle Ground, 10* (2), 39–40.

Titus, Dale N. (2007). Strategies and resources for enhancing the achievement of mobile students. *NASSP Bulletin, 91* (1), 81–97.

United States Department of Education. (2002). The same high standards for migrant students: Holding Title I schools accountable: Executive summary. Washington DC: Author. (ERIC Document Reproduction Service No. ED 467 996).

Walls, Charles A. (2003). Providing highly mobile students with an effective education. New York: ERIC Clearinghouse on Urban Education. (ERIC Document Reproduction Service No. ED 482 918).

Zetlin, Andrea G. & Weinberg, Lois A. (2004). Understanding the plight of foster youth and improving their educational opportunities. *Child Abuse & Neglect, 28* (9), 917–923.

Suggested Activities

1. Read Virginia Rhodes's article "Learning on the Go: Voices of Highly Mobile Urban Students," which is listed in the Appendix of this book. Share your responses to that article.

2. Visit a homeless shelter and ask the students and families how schools and school librarians can help with their educational needs.

3. Ask a school librarian or principal if you can make a display of books or a bibliography of books dealing with highly mobile students.

4. Collaborate with a teacher in a school to present a lesson dealing with highly mobile students (homelessness, foster care, migrant families, or immigrants).

CHAPTER **7**

Students with Gay, Lesbian, Bisexual, or Transgender Orientations

According to Whelan (2006), one of three million gay, lesbian, and bisexual youth are coming out as early as middle school, rather than waiting until they reach college or later life. In the United States, as many as 9 students in every classroom of 30 are in some way affected by sexual orientation issues, either being a sexual minority themselves or having a relative who is among the sexual minority (Savage & Harley, 2009).

Survey results released in 2005 by the Gay, Lesbian and Straight Education Network (GLSEN) revealed that 90 percent of the LGBT (lesbian, gay, bisexual, and transgender) students surveyed had experienced verbal or physical harassment within the previous year, compared to 62 percent of the non-LGBT students. The survey also indicated that LGBT students were less likely to report incidents of victimization to school staff than non-LGBT students (Poland, 2010).

In 2007, GLSEN conducted their fifth National School Climate Survey (NSCS), which is a biennial survey of LGBT students in U.S. secondary schools. The NSCS sample included 6,209 LGBT students from all 50 states and the District of Columbia. Of those completing the survey 626 respondents reported they were enrolled in middle schools. Nine in 10 middle school students (91%) responded that they had experienced harassment at school because of their sexual orientation, and 39 percent reported they had been physically assaulted (punched, kicked, or injured with a weapon) because of their sexual orientation. Many of these middle school students (50%) also reported that they had missed at least one day of school in the previous month because they felt unsafe. Eight out of 10 LGBT middle school students (82%) said they had heard homophobic terms used frequently by students in their schools, and 63 percent reported that they had heard staff make homophobic comments. Many of the middle school students also reported they did not have access to important resources either through their school libraries or through Internet access in their classrooms (Gay, Lesbian and Straight Education Network, 2009).

These startling statistics should be a wake-up call to teachers, administrators, school librarians, and education policy makers. It is clear that not only is there a need to create safer school climates for LGBT students, but school librarians should provide resources in their collections to meet the needs of this special group of students. Additionally, appropriate and accurate information should be included in the curriculum in middle and high schools, and access to informative Internet resources should be provided through school computers.

Definitions

There is sometimes confusion about the language used to discuss sexual orientation and gender identity. In this chapter LGBT will be used as the umbrella category to identify those persons who are considered part of sexual orientation and gender identity minorities. Students in middle and high schools, as well as educators should understand the following terms:

- *lesbian*—females who are attracted to other females
- *gay*—males who are attracted to other males (sometimes used to also include lesbians)
- *bisexual*—persons who are attracted to both males and females
- *transgender*—people whose gender identity does not match their biological sex
- *questioning*—people who are not sure of their sexual orientation or gender identity
- *queer*—an umbrella term used for all LGBT persons (considered offensive in the past, but used today by some LGBT persons to describe themselves)
- *heterosexual or straight*—persons who are attracted only to the opposite sex
- *homophobia*—the fear of gay males and lesbians
- *coming out*—acknowledging one's sexual orientation or gender identity to others
- *outing*—revealing an LGBT person's sexual orientation or gender identity without that person's permission to do so

Unfortunately, there is not much consistency in the language that refers to these minorities, and the language is continually evolving and being debated (Ressler & Chase, 2009).

Legislation

Schools are required to protect all students. Although LGBT persons are not guaranteed the same rights as racial minorities and women under federal statute, the Equal Protection of the Fourteenth Amendment of the U.S. Constitution does protect them. In 1996, a case (*Nabozny v. Podlesny*) was won for gay youth Jamie Nabozny against his school for failing to protect him from antigay harassment and violence.

Other legislative cases that are applicable to gay rights have also been cited in the literature. In the 1982 case *Board of Education, Island Trees (NY) Union Free School District No. 23 v. Steven A. Pico, et al.* the U.S. Supreme Court ruled that a book could not be removed from a library simply because school officials disliked the ideas expressed in it. The U.S. Supreme Court in 1990 supported the rights of gays in the case of *Board of Education of Westside Community Schools v. Mergens* by declaring the 1984 Equal Access Act constitutional. This act requires that public schools that allow noncurricular student-led clubs must provide equal access to all such clubs (Cart & Jenkins, 2006). This last case makes it possible for Gay-Straight Alliances to be created in public schools.

Gay-Straight Alliances, or GSAs, are student-led, school-organized clubs whose purpose is to create safe, accepting environments for all youth, regardless of their sexual orientation or gender identity. GSAs allow LGBT and straight students to cooperatively address issues that affect all students. Some school administrators may balk at allowing students to start GSAs. However, as long as there are noncurricular clubs, such as a Key Club or a chess club, in a public school, the federal law guarantees students the right to have a GSA in that school (American Civil Liberties Union, n.d.).

LGBT Issues in the Curriculum

Reading LGBT-themed literature is probably one of the best ways to combat homophobia in schools. Although it is limited, there is a body of scholarship that has examined the use of LGBT-themed literature in schools, particularly in high school classrooms. Caroline Clark and Mollie Blackburn (2009) discuss their integration of LGBT-themed literature into the curriculum by using book discussion groups made up of both students and adults. They recommend choosing literature that does not just make homosexuality visible, but that also shows LGBT people in gay communities so that young people know that being gay does not mean being alone. They also recommend involving students in making choices of high-quality, pleasurable young adult titles.

High school teacher Jason Zanitsch (2009) uses process drama to overcome the reluctance of students to become emotionally engaged with LGBT characters in literature. The drama activity, which was conceived by a British drama educator, includes a sequence of structured improvisations that explore a central theme. Zanitsch found that using process drama in a classroom engages students on a multitude of levels, and makes it possible for students to investigate issues of sexual orientation and gender identity from multiple perspectives. He uses process drama as a pre-reading activity for books such as Perry Moore's *Hero*, Francesa Lia Block's *Dangerous Angels*, Julie Anne Peter's *Luna*, and Brent Hartinger's *Geography Circle*, all of which include young people who are struggling with the social and personal implications of sexual orientation and gender identity.

The students in Sara Lewis-Bernstein Young's (2009) course in contemporary issues chose homophobia as an issue to investigate. They began the unit by reflecting in their journals on their experiences and beliefs about sexual orientation and homophobia and on what they saw in their schools, homes, and community in regard to this issue. In the classroom they talked about and began to think critically about language, such as the use of the phrase "that's so gay" and "gay rights." Students did not know what some of the terms used to discuss the issue meant so they defined words such as *queer* and *transgender*. They also watched a *Frontline* episode entitled "The Assault on Gay America" and arranged for a panel discussion to hear from LGBT people about their experiences.

Other media that could be used for viewing and discussion in a high school classroom include *Facing Evil*, a documentary with Bill Moyers that addresses discrimination and acts of violence against people, and *Laramie Project*, a movie about the murder of Matthew Shepard, a young gay man from Laramie, Wyoming. Starting and stopping these powerful movies for discussion can provide opportunities for students to express their thoughts and feelings (Roeck, 2008).

Additional ways that teachers can increase multiculturalism in curricula are by discussing sexual orientations in an open manner with neutral language, identifying lesbians and gays of accomplishment, and by having gay studies courses. When teachers introduce texts and images that represent the difficulties that LGBT young people face, as well as the fulfilling lives that gay people can and do have; when sexual and gender minority students are treated with respect; and when all students are provided opportunities to explore their sexual orientation and gender identities through reading, writing, and drama, then a world of possibilities can be opened for LGBT persons, their families, and virtually everyone in a school (Ressler & Chase, 2009).

Organizations and Publications

A number of organizations offer resources and support to LGBT persons, their families, and schools. GLSEN, a national organization which was established in 1990, conducts the surveys mentioned previously and provides numerous resources through their Web site http://www.glsen.org. GLSEN focuses on ensuring safe schools for all students and works to protect students from bullying and harassment. The organization also strives to build the skills of educators so they are able to teach respect for all people.

Parents, Families, and Friends of Lesbians and Gays (PFLAG) is a national non-profit organization with over 500 affiliates throughout the United States. The idea for PFLAG began in 1972, and the first formal meeting took place in 1973 with 20 people attending. Today there are over 200,000 members and supporters of PFLAG. Their vision is to celebrate diversity, including those with diverse sexual orientations and gender identities. More information about PFLAG can be found at http://www.pflag.org.

Lambda, http://www.lambda.org, is a nonprofit organization dedicated to reducing homophobia, inequality, hate crimes, and discrimination. Their Youth Outreach Web site provides opportunities for LGBT youth to interact with others and provides resources for LGBT young people to take care of themselves and make responsible decisions. Another group that provides support, advocacy, information, and resources for LGBT youth is Out-Proud http://www.aboutus.org/Outproud.org.

The American Library Association hosts a Gay, Lesbian, Bisexual, and Transgendered Round Table and is dedicated to serving the needs of LGBT persons, as well as providing free access to information. They sponsor the Stonewall Book Awards, which honor both fiction and nonfiction books for their exceptional merit relating to the LGBT experience. Although the winners sometimes include books appropriate for young people, many of the titles are intended for adults. The ALA Rainbow Project, which is a joint project of the GLBT Round Table and the Social Responsibilities Round Table, creates an annual listing of GLBT books that are recommended specifically for young readers from birth through age 18. More information and access to the recommended bibliographies can be found at http://ala.org/ala/mgrps/rts/glbtrt/rainbow/index.cfm.

In addition, there are other helpful resources, such as *Lesbian and Gay Voices: An Annotated Bibliography and Guide to Literature for Children and Young Adults* (Day, 2000), which includes annotated bibliographies of more that 275 recommended books that feature major and minor lesbian or gay characters. Recommended age levels are provided, as well as indications of the inclusion of strong language and/or explicit sex.

The *Advocate Magazine* publishes news stories relating to the interests of LGBT persons and is available in both print and digital formats. *Out* is another magazine that focuses on the life of gay persons, with subscriptions available in both digital and print formats. The contents of both magazines are not directed specifically to young people, but may be of interest to them.

The Role of the School Librarian

One of the most important roles that school librarians can assume with LGBT students is to make certain they are providing safe and supportive environments. Students need to know that the school library is an open, accepting place for all students, regardless of gender, sexual orientation, ethnicity, race, or any other differences. The school librarian should always model positive, tolerant behavior.

Supporting LGBT Students

There are numerous ways that school librarians can support LGBT students. Probably one of the most important ways to do this is by making certain LGBT resources are displayed throughout the year and easy access to them is provided.

Other ways that school librarians can help provide needed information and a supportive environment for LGBT students are by:

- recommending gay, lesbian, and bisexual writers to students and teachers
- including LGBT-themed books in book talks
- working collaboratively with teachers on lessons or projects that address respect and appreciation for diversity
- becoming an active member of the school's Gay-Straight Alliance
- posting announcements pertaining to LGBT youth clubs or other services
- helping establish in the school district strict antiharassment policies that include sexual orientation and gender identification, if such policies do not already exist
- making certain that LGBT books are easily accessible (cataloging books using subject headings that include terms that are commonly used)
- providing information files about legal issues dealing with LGBT issues

LGBT young people are in need of self-affirmation and opportunities to socialize with other LGBT persons. School librarians can help lessen the feelings of isolation that LGBT students often experience by providing access to responsible Internet resources. Sandra Hughes-Hassell and Alissa Hinckley (2001) list and describe some of these Web sites in an article in the fall 2001 issue of *Journal of Youth Services in Libraries*. School librarians can share such resources by bookmarking sites or providing an annotated bibliography of them.

Literature

During the last decade, there has been a growing amount of LGBT-themed literature produced; thus, school librarians and teachers should not have to search far to find good quality LGBT materials. Many of these books, however, are still challenged in school and public libraries, and some groups actively pursue attempts to have LGBT materials banned from libraries. In 2009, 3 of the top 10 challenged books reported by ALA were challenged because of homosexuality in the books. It is important to keep reviews of LGBT materials when purchasing them for the school library and to consider purchasing materials with literary merit that will be easier to defend in possible challenge cases. Furthermore, school librarians need to make certain that collection development and book challenge policies are in place. Not purchasing LGBT materials because they might be controversial is denying information to students, and it violates the very principles on which librarianship is based. It is also important to remember that legislation is on the side of providing young people access to LGBT materials.

The following are some LGBT-themed books that in past years have won awards or been listed on best book lists:

Alsenas, Linas. (2008). *Gay America: Struggle for equality.* New York: Amulet.
> This nonfiction work covers the history of gay and lesbians during the past 125 years. Numerous black-and-white and full-color photos accompany the very readable text. The book was named to many outstanding book lists, including ALA's Rainbow List.

Bauer, Marion Dane. (Ed.). (2004). *Am I blue? Coming out of the silence.* New York: HarperCollins.
> Sixteen well-known authors of young adult fiction write original short stories of the experiences of gay or lesbian young people or having gay parents. The book also contains one-page biographies of each of the authors.

Block, Francesca Lia. (1995). *Baby Be-Bop.* New York: HarperCollins.
> Dirk McDonald, a 16-year-old boy living in Los Angeles with his grandmother, comes to terms with being gay, but struggles with how to tell his grandmother. Dirk is one of the characters from Block's earlier popular novel *Weetzie Bat. Baby Be-Bop* has been frequently challenged, but a lawsuit in 1999 in Wisconsin returned the book to the shelves of school libraries.

Cameron, Peter. (2007). *Some day this pain will be useful to you.* New York: Farrar, Straus and Giroux.
> James, an 18-year-old gay boy, feels alienated from the world and experiences much loneliness as he works in his mother's Manhattan art gallery while he decides if he wants to go to college. The story is told with both compassion and humor.

Crutcher, Chris. (1991). *Athletic shorts.* New York: Greenwillow.
> Five of the six short stories in this collection include previous athletic protagonists from Crutcher's novels. All the young people are grappling with difficult situations in their lives.

Garden, Nancy. (2007). *Annie on my mind.* New York: Farrar, Straus and Giroux.
> This is the paperback edition of the original book published in 1982. This classic in young adult literature deals with two 17-year-old girls who meet at the New York Metropolitan of Art and become friends. Their friendship eventually develops into romantic love. This award-winning book has been challenged numerous times in school and public libraries.

Garden, Nancy. (2007). *Hear us out: Lesbian and gay stories of struggle, progress and hope, 1950–present.* New York: Farrar, Straus and Giroux.
> Garden's book is a unique combination of fiction and history. Each decade is given its own section, beginning with the 1950s. Garden summarizes the experiences of

gay and lesbian young people during each decade, adding her own insights, and some of her well-written stories. The book appears on ALA's 2008 Rainbow Book List.

Hartinger, Brent. (2003). *Geography club.* New York: Harper Teen.
Four closeted high school boys are afraid to start a Gay-Straight Alliance so begin an after-school club that they call the Geography Club because it sounds so boring and nerdy that no one else will want to join. The club turns out to be a place where they can discuss their concerns and begin the journey of accepting themselves.

Howe, James. (2005). *Totally Joe.* New York: Atheneum.
As a school assignment, 13-year-old Joe writes an alphabiography—life from A to Z, in which he reveals much about his life including the fact that he is gay. The book was selected for the 2006 ALA Notable Children's Books.

Huegel, Kelly. (2003). *GLBTQ: The survival guide for queer and questioning teens.* Minneapolis: Free Spirit.
The basics of GLTBQ are discussed in contemporary language in this book, which covers all the aspects of being GLTBQ and provides sound, practical advice and encouragement. The author includes numerous references to other LGBT resources.

Kerr, M. E. (2004). *Deliver us from Evie.* New York: HarperCollins.
Teenager Parr Burman's older sister Evie had always been different, wearing boys' clothing and fixing farm machinery, despite her mother's attempts to make her more ladylike. The story is told through the perspective of Parr, a high school junior who hopes Evie will help keep the family farm going with their father so Parr will not have to do so. Evie, however, leaves the farm to live with the daughter of the small town's banker. The book has won several awards, including being selected as one of ALA's Best Books for Young Adults in 1995.

LaRochelle, David. (2005). *Absolutely positively not.* New York: Arthur A. Levine.
LaRochelle introduces readers to 16-year-old Steven Narski who tries to convince everyone he is not gay by taking part in several events, including inventing a girlfriend named Kelly. The story is humorous, but presented in such a way that readers will sympathize with Steven. The book won several awards, including the 2006 Sid Fleischman Humor Award.

Levithan, David. (2003). *Boy meets boy.* New York: Alfred A. Knopf.
Paul falls in love with Nathan, but he becomes confused when his ex-boyfriend Kyle comes between them. The story is fresh and funny and shows that both gay and straight teens have similar questioning thoughts about dating and love.

Myracle, Lauren. (2003). *Kissing Kate.* New York: Dutton's Children's Books.
One summer night at a party Kate, a drunk 16-year-old girl, leans in and kisses her longtime best friend Lissa, who kisses her back. Kate then begins to avoid Lissa, and Lissa becomes confused about their friendship and her own sexuality. With the help of an unexpected new friend Lissa is able to come to terms with who she is and who she wants to be.

Peters, Julie Anne. (2004). *Luna.* New York: Little, Brown.
Regan's brother Liam does not like being the person that he is during the day so he chooses his female namesake Luna, and at night, with the help of his sister's

clothes and makeup, he transforms himself into the beautiful girl he would like to be. This story of a transgender teen is told through the eyes of his sympathetic sister. Peters's book was a finalist for the 2004 National Book Award for Young People's Literature.

Ryan, Sara. (2001). *Empress of the world.* New York: St. Martin's Press.
Fifteen-year-old Nicola goes away to attend classes at a summer institute for the gifted and falls in love with another girl. However, this confuses Nicola because she has been attracted only to boys in the past. This is one of the few teen novels that deal with bisexuality.

Sanchez, Alex. (2001). *Rainbow Boys.* New York: Simon & Schuster.
This book takes an honest look at the life of three gay teenagers, Jason, Nelson, and Kyle, who are seniors attending the same high school. The book, which won several awards, is the first of a trilogy; the others are *Rainbow High* (2003) and *Rainbow Road* (2005).

Sanchez, Alex. (2004). *So hard to say.* New York: Simon & Schuster.
Frederick, a shy 13-year-old, moves from Wisconsin to Los Angeles and is be-friended by some Latina girls at his middle school. He and Xio become good friends, but when she wants more than friendship, Frederick realizes he is more attracted to Victor, the captain of the soccer team. The book won numerous awards, including the 2004 Lambda Literary Award.

Tamaki, Mariko. (2008). *Skim.* Illus. Jillian Tamaki. Toronto: Groundwood.
This graphic novel set in Toronto in 1994 is the story of 16-year-old Skim who, like her best friend Lisa, is an outsider in a private girls' school. Skim develops a crush on Ms. Archer, her English teacher. The story deals with the innermost thoughts and feelings of a teenaged outsider. The book has won numerous awards, including a Best Illustrated Children's Book Award from the *New York Times.*

Woodson, Jacqueline. (2008). *After Tupac and D Foster.* New York: Putnam.
Set in Queens, New York, in the mid-1990s two "almost" 12-year-old girls befriend D, a foster child who roams into their neighborhood. They all become friends during the summer, especially after their idol Tupac Shakur is shot but survives. The moving story explores issues of homosexuality, homophobia in an African-American community, and coming of age. The book is a 2008 Newbery Award Honor Book.

This chapter has dealt primarily with materials for teens who have identified themselves as LGBT or questioning persons; however, it is also important for elementary school librarians to include in their collections materials that represent diverse families. Children need to see their families (whether those families include two male parents or two female parents) represented in books. Although there are still a limited number of LGBT-themed picture books available, the number of titles is increasing. Publishers are in the business of selling their materials; thus, when books seem as though they will be controversial and not be purchased by libraries, companies are less likely to publish them. Most LGBT-themed books for children, even if they are considered high-quality literature, go out of print fairly quickly (Casement, 2002). Some of these titles, however, are becoming more available in both school and public libraries. Three of the most recognized titles are Michael Willhoite's

Daddy's Roommate (1990), Leslea Newman's *Heather Has Two Mommies*, and *And Tango Makes Three* (2005) by Justin Richardson and Peter Parnell. All three books have faced numerous challenges and have been banned from libraries in some communities. Discussion of other LGBT-themed titles to include in library collections for children can be found in Kay Chick's article (2008), which appears in *Bookbird*.

Conclusions

Even though the level of tolerance in regard to the visibility and acceptance of sexual orientation minorities has increased in the past several years, LGBT students continue to experience verbal and physical harassment in schools. It is important that all students have safe school environments where they can freely express and examine their identities. Educators should also create opportunities and resources for straight students to learn to understand and support their LGBT peers. LGBT students want and need support and information. Teachers can assist by including LGBT-themed materials and issues in the curriculum. School librarians can contribute to meeting the needs of LGBT students by acting as supportive adults and developing and maintaining library collections that contain high-quality informational and fiction resources that deal with sexual orientations and gender identity. Education at every level (student, staff, and faculty) needs to be increased so there is more awareness about the issues and misinformation that surround sexual orientation and gender identity. Moreover, it is essential that all adults in a school internalize an attitude of respect for differences in students; until this is accomplished they will not be able to transmit this respect to their students.

References

American Civil Liberties Union (n.d.). *Start a gay-straight alliance.* Retrieved from http://gbge.aclu.org/schools/start-gay-straight-alliance

Cart, Michael, & Jenkins, Christine A. (2006). *The heart has its reasons: Young adult literature with gay/lesbian/queer content, 1969–2004.* Lanham, MD: Scarecrow Press.

Casement, Rose. (2002). Breaking the silence: The stories of gay and lesbian people in children's literature. *New Advocate, 15* (3), 205–213.

Chick, Kay. (2008). Fostering an appreciation for all kinds of families: Picturebooks with gay and lesbian themes. *Bookbird, 46* (1), 15–22.

Clark, Caroline T., & Blackburn, Mollie V. (2009). Reading LGBT-themed literature with young people: What's possible? *English Journal, 98* (4), 25–32.

Day, Frances. (2000). *Lesbian and gay voices: An annotated bibliography and guide to literature for children and young adults.* Westport, CT: Greenwood Press.

Gay, Lesbian and Straight Education Network (GLSEN). (2009). *The experiences of lesbian, gay, bisexual and transgender middle school students: Findings from the 2007 National School Climate Survey. Research brief.* Retrieved from http://www.glsen.org/cgi-bin/iowa/all/home/index.html

Hughes-Hassell, Sandra, & Hinckley, Alissa. (2001). Reaching out to lesbian, gay, bisexual, and transgender youth. *Journal of Youth Services in Libraries, 15* (1), 39–41.

Poland, Scott. (2010). LGBT students need support at school. *District Administration, 46* (1), 44.

Ressler, Paula & Chase, Becca. (2009). Sexual identity and gender variance: Meeting the educational challenges. *English Journal, 98* (4), 15–22.

Roeck, Kathryn. (2008). Exploring how to change stereotypical attitudes toward students who are LGBT. *Democracy & Education, 18* (1), 53–56.

Savage, Todd A., & Harley, Debra A. (2009). A place at the blackboard LGBTIQ. *Multicultural Education, 16* (4), 2–9.

Whelan, Debra Lau. (2006). Out and ignored: Why are so many school libraries reluctant to embrace gay teens. *School Library Journal, 52* (1), 46–50.

Young, Sara Lewis-Bernstein. (2009). Breaking the silence: Critical literacy and social action. *English Journal, 98* (4), 109–115.

Zanitsch, Jason. (2009). Playing in the margins: Process drama as a prereading strategy with LGBT YA literature. *English Journal, 98* (4), 85–91.

Suggested Activities

1. Find a school that has a Gay-Straight Alliance and ask if you can attend one of their meetings. In a reflective report, describe the meeting, including the topics and issues discussed.

2. Contact a school librarian and ask if the librarian would like you to create a pathfinder of LGBT materials for the library.

3. Research some of the court cases that deal with LGBT student issues and write a paper on your findings.

4. Collaborate with a teacher or school librarian to teach a lesson that deals with respect for all types of diversity, including persons with diverse sexual orientations or gender identities.

Learning More about Special Groups of Students

Three special groups of students were discussed in this section—autistic students, young people from highly mobile families, and students with lesbian, gay, bisexual, or transgender orientations. There are certainly other groups of students who deserve special attention from teachers, administrators, and school librarians.

One can research groups of students having the following characteristics in order to learn about their special needs and how those needs can be addressed in the classroom and school library to provide the best learning environments for the students.

- At-risk backgrounds
- Attention deficit disorders
- Chronic illnesses
- Emotional disabilities
- English as a second language
- Gifted
- Lack of motivation
- Learning disabilities
- Mental disabilities
- Physical disabilities
- Reluctant or resistive reading habits
- Talents in the performing arts

Educational literature contains numerous articles and books on these groups of students. In addition, there are frequently national and state associations and agencies that address the needs of special students. Conducting a search online will also bring up several Web sites that provide information about students with these characteristics. Since several of these groups of students are in educational programs that are designated as "inclusive" or "mainstreamed classes," researching those terms can also prove beneficial in learning more about these special students.

Educational Trends and the School Librarian

Public education in the United States has come under much criticism in the past few decades. Confidence in public schools has declined dramatically. Comparisons to other nations show American students to be only average in math and science. Parents, employers, taxpayers, and students themselves have called for renewed efforts to "fix" public education. Many nonprofit organizations and groups of parents have assembled to try to come up with solutions to the problems. Some reformers have emphasized the need for higher standards for students and more accountability for schools. Others have debated the use of various methods of teaching, such as literature-based reading versus phonics, or using calculators in math classes.

The need for more adequate and equitable funding for public schools has also been at the center of educational discussion. The public, however, seems fairly divided on the topic of whether more money will improve the schools. Another area of educational reform has dealt with the idea of letting the free market improve public education. Advocates of this idea believe public education has not improved because it does not have competition. They encourage the creation of charter schools and the use of school vouchers that can be used by parents for public or private schools. Other parents have chosen to homeschool their children, rather than sending them to organized schools.

It is true that most Americans want action to improve the public school system and there have been several possible solutions introduced by the federal and state governments. The following chapters deal with some recent educational trends and reforms in K–12 schools—Web 2.0 applications, distance education, and inclusion. All three of these trends have greatly expanded, with currently no indications of slowing down or changing despite the fact that they have caused controversy. The chapters deal with these controversies, as well as defining some confusing terms, discussing benefits and challenges, and describing the roles of school librarians with the trends.

CHAPTER 8

Web 2.0

Web 2.0, a term coined in 2004, includes both new and emerging Web-based tools that people are able to access using the browsers on their computers (Solomon & Schrum, 2007). Many of the tools are free and some are social in nature, thus promoting collaboration and self-expression. Web 2.0 promotes three functions or practices: participation, collaboration, and distribution (Knobel & Wilber, 2009). Using Web 2.0 applications, people can read, write, post comments, converse, collaborate, create, and critique online. Unlike Web 1.0 where information moved in only one direction (from Web sites to the user), Web 2.0 is two-way where anyone with an Internet browser can become a contributor or author with very little technical knowledge. Web 2.0 is having a profound effect on society, not only in the United States, but globally as people are able to generate content, interact, and share information across borders.

The following additional terms that are sometimes found in articles or books dealing with Web 2.0 are defined by Rosen and Nelson (2008) and can help readers better understand some of the Web 2.0 tools and concepts:

- *blogs or Weblogs*—online journals that consist of posts in reverse chronological order, with the most recent post appearing at the top of the Web page
- *digital immigrants*—persons who acquire the use of digital technologies, much like second-language acquisition
- *digital natives*—persons who have grown up with digital and cyber technologies
- *Education 2.0*—the use of digital tools in both teaching and learning
- *Faculty 2.0*—teachers who are using Web 2.0 applications in their classrooms
- *NetGen or Net Generation*—a phrase to identify the new generation that is comfortable using digital technologies
- *rich-site summary or RSS*—news feeds that bring to the user the latest updates on Weblogs, wikis, newspapers, or other online sites by aggregating the updates for the user
- *wikis*—Web sites that can be edited online as long as the user has access privileges (e.g., *Wikipedia*)

Technology is at the center of the majority of young people's lives. It is second nature for today's students, and they accept the new technologies without questions. While at one time new technologies and their uses were introduced by adults to students, this is no longer the typical scenario. Young people are not waiting for permission or instructions to use Web 2.0 tools; they are discovering and using the emergent technologies.

Controversy

While some educators feel that Web 2.0 tools are critical to 21st-century learning, just as many are resistive and do not want the technology devices and applications available in their classrooms and libraries. David Loertscher (2009) describes three types of school districts that seem to have emerged in their dealings with Web 2.0:

- The Just Say No Crowd—districts that operate out of fear and lock down any access to Web 2.0 with heavy filters
- The Inside the Firewall Group—districts that build a strong firewall, but try to pull into the internal space selected Web 2.0 applications, such as internal wikis and blogs
- The Wide Open Group—districts that apply a light filter and are friendly to teachers and school librarians who want to access tools that have potential for teaching and learning

Barriers

Fear of Web 2.0 is a major barrier that exists not only with educators, but also with parents and the general public. According to Solomon and Schrum (2007), 71 percent of parents believe that schools should bear the primary responsibility for student safety on the Internet, and 49 percent of parents think that government and law enforcement agencies should carry much of the responsibility for children's safety on the Internet. Thus, the U.S. federal government addressed parent concerns by passing the Children's Internet Protection Act (CIPA) in December 2000. CIPA mandates that school libraries receiving E-rate funding for Internet access or internal connections, or those receiving Library Services Technology Act (LSTA) funds are required to install filters on any of their computers that have Internet access. This, in turn, has set up a barrier that stifles the use of many Web 2.0 applications. Some school administrators feel that blocking Web 2.0 sites en masse is easier and safer than identifying the tools that might have educational value. They fear use of Web 2.0 will result in major lawsuits or bad press (Underwood, 2009).

Because of the huge amount of information available online, students need direction and assistance in evaluating the information. Guiding students in this task can be both time-consuming and challenging for teachers. Many teachers complain that with the huge pressures that are put upon them by high-stakes testing, they do not have time to learn about Web 2.0 tools or to use them with their students.

Additionally, some teachers fear that they will lose control of their materials, methods, and students. It is true that learning with Web 2.0 tools is student-centered, with teachers often serving more as facilitators of learning, rather than doing actual instruction.

The Internet, social networking, cell phones, and laptops have magnified the gap between teachers and students. Many of today's students are more tech-savvy than their teachers, which, in turn, can be intimidating to some teachers. The devices are often seen as disruptive and unsafe. Banning the use of these devices and Web 2.0 resources in a school is thus favored by many teachers and administrators.

Benefits

While there are challenges to using Web 2.0 applications in education, the benefits are plentiful:

- Students tend to be more engaged in learning when they are able to use well-chosen technology resources.
- Many of the Web 2.0 tools are free and can be cost-saving to schools.
- The tools are generally easy to use and require little instruction.
- Students learn how to collaborate and gain team skills.
- Groups are formed around common interests where the participants can collate information and share it with others.
- Students are able to create work, post their work, and receive feedback from others (not only from a teacher).
- Through greater participation, students are able to take ownership of their work.
- Students feel that their voices are heard and their ideas matter.
- Students are able to answer questions posed to them and also create their own questions.
- Hyperlinked writing makers it easier for teachers and students to verify information in student work.
- Projects that reach across borders create a sense of community, sharing, and learning about other cultures.
- The Web 2.0 applications support multiple learning styles.
- Many Web 2.0 tools allow for experimentation and thus nurture creativity and innovation.

Teaching with Web 2.0

Learning spaces have traditionally been physical spaces, such as classrooms or libraries. However, with the introduction of new technologies into schools the idea of what constitutes a learning environment has changed. The spaces where students learn today in school are not only in physical rooms. Using the Internet and Web 2.0 resources, learning now goes beyond the classroom, across state lines, and even into countries around the world.

Learning has also become more collaborative and creative. The values of collaboration and creativity in the workplace have become increasingly important in recent years as people work across geographic and cultural borders. In order to prepare students for their future careers, teachers are recognizing the importance of both collaboration and creativity. They are having students work in groups in their classrooms and beyond their classrooms. Educators are locating the online applications that make it possible for students to more easily collaborate and produce creative products.

Blogging software was the first Web 2.0 tool to hit the market in 1998. Blogs slowly made their way into mainstream education and are frequently used today by educators. Using blog software, teachers can post assignments or subject content, and students are able to add comments, ask questions, and share their research.

Many teachers have also found educational applications for wikis, photo-sharing software, and audio and video digital tools. Some examples of their use in classrooms are the following:

- Compile and present a local history study by embedding archival photos, creating hyperlinked pages that focus on different aspects of local history, and posting oral history interviews of podcasts they have created (Knobel & Wilber, 2009).
- Develop literacy skills in literature circles where students can choose what they read and through blogs discuss and collaborate in an inquiry-based framework (DeVault, 2009).
- Create a blog about Africa by assigning a different African country for each student to research and then adding information to the blog (Byrne, 2009).
- Join the Kites Around the World international project where students can learn how to build different types of kites, explore kite design, and contribute videos of themselves flying their kites (New Media Consortium, 2010).
- Create an internal YouTube museum of student creations, similar to a school yearbook (Loertscher, 2009).

Some teachers have also used the popular attraction of games in their classrooms by taking advantage of online collaborative multiplayer games that draw on problem solving and constructing knowledge. Many of the games lend themselves well to the curriculum. The Global Kids Gaming Initiative uses online games to promote digital literacy skills, global awareness, and citizenship. Information about the initiative can be found at the Global Kids Web site, which can be accessed at http://www.globalkids.org/?id=21.

Mary J. Johnson (2009) provides many interesting and useful examples of classroom applications of Web 2.0 in her book *Primary Source Teaching the Web 2.0 Way K–12*. Other examples can be found online by searching the Web using the terms "Web 2.0 lesson plans."

The Role of the School Librarian

School librarians have always been leaders in technology and other forms of innovation. Thus, it is no different with Web 2.0. School librarians are leaders in the use of collaborative tools of Web 2.0, such as blogs and wikis. They realize Web 2.0 tools can assist in meeting AASL's *Standards for the 21st-Century Learner*. Collaboration is one of the defining characteristics of 21st-century learning and is emphasized by AASL and also by the International Society for Technology in Education (ISTE).

Student Online Safety

Even if young people are more proficient with Web 2.0 tools than some teachers, it is up to adults to guide students. CIPA regulations require schools to provide online safety training. Adults can use their wisdom and experience to suggest what personal information is safe to share and what is appropriate to post online. Students also need to be able to recognize inappropriate online solicitation and what behaviors may be potentially risky. They should be warned against cyber bullying and what to do if they are victims of such harassment. Student accountability and responsibility need to be emphasized. Cyber safety education can be provided through workshops collaboratively led by teachers and school librarians. There are also Web sites, such as Staysafeonline.org, that provide K–12 curriculum for developing programs for safe and ethical online behavior.

The use of Web 2.0 tools calls for a student code of ethics that should be read and signed by all students using the applications in a school. Many schools developed Internet policies when students and teachers began to use Internet in their schools; however, those policies may need to be readdressed to make certain that they include the use of Web 2.0 tools that are available through the school's Internet access. Consequences for misuse of the Internet also need to be included in an Internet policy, and consistent application of the consequences is essential.

Professional Development

School librarians need to stay abreast of Web 2.0 tools and not be fearful of their use. In many cases, particularly for librarians who have been in the field for several years, this means taking advantage of professional development opportunities. State, regional, and national conferences provide many sessions that relate to new technologies. Professional journals are including numerous articles and sometimes entire issues that deal with Web 2.0. Scholars and practitioners have written books on the topic and have shared their experiences and expertise. By accessing and using some of the Web 2.0 tools librarians can also become familiar with the applications.

After school librarians become knowledgeable about Web 2.0 resources, they then should take the leadership in schools to help teachers become acquainted with tools that can be used with their students. The following are some suggested resources that school librarians can share in professional development sessions:

- **Blogger,** http://www.blogger.com: a free blogging host that can be used for posting content and comments
- **Delicious,** http://www.delicious.com: a free social, Internet bookmarking service that allows users to have access to their bookmarks from any computer
- **Google Docs,** http: docs.google.com: a secure group of applications that allow students and teachers to create documents, share calendars, send e-mail messages, create Web pages, and perform various other tasks
- **PB Wiki,** http://www.pbwiki.com: a safe, easy-to-use wiki that can be used for collaboration
- **Toondo,** http://www.toondo.com: a tool for creating original comic strips
- **Twitter,** http://twitter.com: a service for users to communicate through quick, frequent exchanges
- **Vimeo,** http://www.vimeo.com: a secure video-sharing tool that supports high-definition video, comments, and storage
- **Voicethread,** http://voicethread.com: a user-generated content hosting site that makes it possible for users to leave audio and video comments on posts
- **Writeboard,** http://www.writeboard.com: an application that is used to share work and collaborate with others

- **Zoho,** http://zoho.com: a comprehensive collaborative environment in which users can work with others on documents, chat, send e-mail messages, and have Web conferences
- **Zotero,** http://www.zotero.org: an easy-to-use Firefox extension to help users collect, manage, and cite sources

Conclusions

What has happened in recent years with the use of Web 2.0 is not just a technological revolution, but even more, a social revolution. Schools are being faced with how to incorporate into education the changes that have occurred in this social revolution. Web 2.0 offers educators new teaching and learning tools and changes the ways that students and teachers interact. Educators and policy makers have many concerns when considering the use of Web 2.0 applications in schools. These include online safety of young people, filters mandated by CIPA, loss of teacher control of learning, and disruption of classrooms with electronic devices. Regardless of these concerns, many educators are realizing the importance of Web 2.0 tools in preparing their students for the future; thus, teachers are incorporating them into instruction and student learning in their schools. School librarians can play significant roles in the use of Web 2.0 tools by helping develop Internet policies and student ethics codes for Web 2.0, keeping abreast of emerging technologies, and leading professional development Web 2.0 workshops for teachers. While there are many advantages that Web 2.0 offers for schools and students, it is important to remember that human connections and quality teachers, including knowledgeable school librarians, cannot be replaced by technology.

References

Byrne, Richard. (2009). The effect of Web 2.0 on teaching and learning. *Teacher Librarian, 37* (2), 50–53.

DeVault, Nancy. (2009). Literature circles in library class. *Library Media Connection, 28* (1), 24–25.

Johnson, Mary J. (2009). *Primary source teaching the Web 2.0 way K–12*. Columbus, OH: Linworth.

Knobel, Michele, & Wilber, Dana. (2009). Let's talk 2.0. *Educational Leadership, 66* (6), 20–24.

Loertscher, David V. (2009). Access to technology in transition. *Teacher Librarian, 36* (5), 46–47.

New Media Consortium. (2010). *The 2010 horizon report: K–12 edition*. Retrieved from http://www.nmc.org/pdf/2010-Horizon-Report.pdf

Rosen, Dina & Nelson, Charles. (2008). *Computers in the schools, 25* (3/4), 211–225.

Solomon, Gwen, & Schrum, Lynne. (2007). *Web 2.0: New tools, new schools*. Washington, DC: International Society for Technology in Education.

Underwood, Linda. (2009). What is a school librarian to do? *School Library Monthly, 26* (1), 14–16.

Suggested Activities

1. Explore some Web 2.0 applications and share what you learned with other students or librarians.

2. Create an original lesson plan using a Web 2.0 tool.

3. Observe students using Web 2.0 in a classroom or school library. Share your observations in an informal written paper.

4. Interview some school administrators regarding their opinions about the use of Web 2.0 in education. Report your questions and the administrators' responses in a written document.

CHAPTER 9

Distance Education

The development of recent technology has dramatically changed the ways in which people communicate, learn, and engage with others. The result in education has been a huge increase in distance education, both in institutions of higher learning and in K–12 settings. Huett, Moller, Foshay, and Coleman (2008) note:

> What we are witnessing with the current evolution of distance education and the technologies that support it is nothing less than the single most important reorganization of how we will engage learners since we started to gather students together in school buildings. (pp. 65–66)

K–12 Web-based learning began in 1996 and is a relatively new field that is estimated to be growing 30 percent annually (International Association for K–12 Online Learning, n.d.). A study released in 2005 by the National Center for Education Statistics indicated that nearly a third of public school districts had students enrolled in distance education courses in 2002–2003. As of September 2009, 45 states had significant supplemental or full-time online programs, or both. Twenty-four states, plus Washington, DC have statewide full-time online schools (Evergreen Education Group, 2009). In some small school districts interactive video is the technology that is often cited as a primary instructional delivery system, but larger school districts generally utilize Web-based systems. This chapter deals with primarily computer-based distance education.

There are numerous reasons that K–12 distance education is increasing. In 2009 the Sloan Consortium (2009), an institutional and professional organization committed to quality online education, estimated that more than one million K–12 students in public schools were enrolled in online or blended courses during the 2007–2008 academic school year. The majority of these were at the high school level. In the Sloan Consortium's survey of 867 K–12 public school districts, administrators cited the following reasons for perceiving that online and blended courses are important:

- Meeting the needs of specific groups of students
- Offering courses not otherwise available at the schools
- Offering Advanced Placement or college-level courses

- Permitting students who failed courses to take them again
- Reducing scheduling conflicts for students

They also reported that the major providers for the courses were postsecondary institutions, state virtual schools within the district's home state, independent vendors, and education service agencies.

Definitions

Distance education is described in various ways including *distance learning*, *e-learning*, *Web-based instruction*, *virtual schools*, and *online learning*. The terms are sometimes confusing, but they are basically interchangeable. Schlosser and Simonson (2002) provide the following definition of distance education in a book published by the Association for Educational Communications and Technology: "Institution-based, formal education where the learning group is separated, and where interactive telecommunications systems are used to connect learners, resources, and instructors" (p. 1). In the third edition of their book, Schlosser & Simonson (2010) note that the term *virtual schools* has become popular recently in defining distance education. The United States Distance Learning Association (n.d.) defines distance education as: "The acquisition of knowledge and skills through mediated information and instruction, encompassing all technologies and other forms of learning at a distance."

Many terms have emerged to describe different types of distance education. In a report sponsored by the Sloan Consortium, Allen and Seaman (2006) developed the following specific definitions:

- *Online:* Course where most or all of the content is delivered online. At least 80 percent of seat time is replaced by online activity.
- *Blended/hybrid:* Course that blends online and face-to-face delivery. Between 30 and 79 percent of the content is delivered online.
- *Web-facilitated:* Course that uses Web-based technology to facilitate a face-to-face course. Between 1 and 29 percent of the content is delivered online.

There are three dominant methods of delivery in virtual schooling—independent, asynchronous, and synchronous. A course that is considered independent is very similar to a traditional correspondence course except that a computer is used by the student in the learning experience. Students in this type of independent situation are generally teaching themselves or being assisted by parents with minimal involvement from teachers, while the virtual school provides materials for the students (Barbour & Reeves, 2009).

The asynchronous method of delivery is more common among the statewide virtual schools. In this method students interact with the curriculum, turn in assignments, and receive feedback from teachers through the course management system or by phone. Feedback includes how the students can improve their work. Sometimes a textbook is used for such courses in addition to online course content. Discussion boards are often used in asynchronous courses so students can interact with each other, as well as with teachers.

In the synchronous method of delivery, students and their teacher all meet at the same time. Depending on the software that is used, only one person or multiple people can participate (speak) at the same time. Instant messaging is sometimes used so multiple persons can participate simultaneously in the discussions. Teachers are able to assign students to groups that can work together; also a teacher can assign the moderator control over to a student so the student can present materials within the virtual classroom (Barbour & Reeves, 2009).

Controversy

Just as the No Child Left Behind Act (NCLB) has affected curriculum and special groups of students so has it had an impact on distance education. The act requires states to offer alternative schooling options to students attending schools that fail to make adequate yearly progress (APY). Some states and school districts see distance education as a viable option for choice. Teacher shortages, overcrowded schools, and the rapid growth in student populations are cited as motivational factors for the rise in site-based distance education (Huett, Moller, Foshay, & Coleman, 2008).

Most of the emphasis on virtual schooling has been at the high school level where online high schools have been able to expand course offerings to students, as well as serve the needs of special groups of students. Among the more controversial examples of online learning are the virtual charter schools, which offer distance education learning to public school students, while at the same time operating independently of local school districts. Huerta, d'Entremont, and Gonzalez (2006) have identified two types of charter schools that offer distance education: home-school charter schools that require parents to serve as primary educators and cyber-charter schools that offer computer-based learning with teachers filling the roles of educational facilitators. Politicians, educators, and parents have raised objections relating to the organizational structure of cyber schools and the routing of public funds to charter schools.

Rice (2006) reports that policy makers often do not understand online learning for K–12 schools. Thus, the policy makers apply policies meant for physical brick-and-mortar schools to online programs. The quality of online programs is usually measured with the same indicators used for traditional K–12 programs—academic performance, student retention, and satisfaction. Rice suggests that the effectiveness of distance education depends more on who is teaching, who is learning, and how learning is accomplished, rather than the medium used to deliver courses.

Benefits

Numerous benefits for distance education have been touted in recent years. These include advantages for students, teachers, administrators, and parents:

- Students are able to work at their own pace and practice as needed.
- The specific needs and learning styles of students can be met.
- Students who are not able to attend school for a variety of reasons can take the courses that they need or desire.
- Students in rural settings or in small schools are able to take courses that are not offered at their schools.
- Students are able to take Advanced Placement courses and other college-level courses.
- Students who fail courses are able to take remedial courses.

- Students are able to take courses with students from other geographic and cultural settings and receive the perspectives of those students.
- In asynchronous courses shy students or students who need more "think time" are able to participate more fully in online discussions.
- There is flexibility in time for both the teacher and students in independent or asynchronous courses.
- Teachers potentially have more opportunity to have greater contact with students who are not normally communicative in face-to-face classrooms.
- Administrators can ensure that course content is aligned to standards.
- Distance education is a way to offer more equitable distribution of educational resources.
- Parents are able to see the assignments, readings, and resources available to their children.

Challenges

One of the major challenges of distance education in K–12 initiatives is that the classes are often made up of highly heterogeneous groups of students. K–12 distance education learners include students who are being homeschooled, living in rural areas, have social commitments, are hospitalized or homebound, who require flexible hours because of employment, are incarcerated, are traveling, have behavior problems in regular classrooms, or are in need of courses not offered in their local schools. Thus, the instructional design parameters for this diverse audience of students are challenging, and many issues need to be taken into consideration.

Other factors that can prove to be challenging include:

- Generally there are high start-up costs for virtual schooling.
- Accreditation of some virtual schools may be problematic.
- There has not been a wholesale acceptance of distance education by the general public.
- There is a high dropout rate in some virtual schooling.
- Some students may not have access to computers or Internet at their homes.
- Courses taught through asynchronous instruction may offer few opportunities for personal interaction; thus, students can feel isolated.
- Students have little opportunity for social development in distance learning.
- Some students do not have the motivation or enough self-direction to succeed in distance education.

Distance education is not looked upon favorably by all educators, including many of those in both higher institutions of learning and in K–12 schools. Often faculty members feel that there is not enough training for them to be successful instructors in distance education programs. Thus, more attention and resources for professional development for online instruction is essential.

Research Studies

Unfortunately, very little research currently exists on online learning in K–12 schools. Implementation of distance learning has actually been accomplished in K–12 schools with a limited research base. Often implementation in K–12 educational settings drew on studies from adult distance education and policies. Of the research studies that have been conducted on K–12 programs, most have examined the effectiveness of online learning at the high school level, comparing face-to-face classroom instruction with online instruction. In these studies it appears that there are no significant differences in the student achievements between online learning and learning in face-to-face classes. There are similar findings in the adult studies of distance education (Rice, 2006).

Another area of research in K–12 distance education has focused on examining the qualities and characteristics of the learning experience, including the characteristics of student learners. Again the studies include an analysis of student achievement. Through these research studies it has been determined that many factors coexist in promoting student success in distance education. Learner autonomy and student responsibility are two characteristics of successful distance education that have been mentioned in studies. Research also provides evidence that teacher quality and a high degree of student-teacher interaction are important in the success of students in Web-based distance education (Rice, 2006).

Some studies and models have been designed to predict which students are most likely to be successful in virtual high school courses. In their study Robyler and Marshall (2002/2003) found the following to be indicators that predicted student success in distance education learning: self-motivation, ability to structure one's own learning, technology experience, a positive attitude toward learning, access to technology, previous distance learning experience, and outside school responsibilities.

By using a national survey, Archambault and Crippen (2009) were able to examine the demographic nature and experiences of 596 K–12 online teachers from 25 states in the United States. They found that online teachers are experienced teachers in the traditional classroom and have advanced degrees. Results also indicated that the respondents were motivated, innovative, eager to learn, and valued the opportunities and advantages of online distance education. Archambault and Crippen (2009) recommend more research on the content of online courses; instructional, interaction methodologies, and assessment strategies used with classes; how experiences of traditional classroom teaching impact online teaching; and the hiring, evaluation, and professional development of online teachers.

The question of how effective distance learning can be for younger children has not been addressed in research. It is possible that students younger than high school age require more supervision, simpler instructions, and more reinforcement than older students (Huett et al., 2008). Further research is needed on how to successfully deliver materials to these younger students. Other areas that need continued research are the expansion of prediction instruments that can reliably identify student success in distance learning and being able to determine the skills, motivation, and characteristics that are needed to improve the experiences of virtual school students (Barbour & Reeves, 2009).

The Role of the School Librarian

Expecting teachers to be excellent instructors, as well as content experts, distance education instructional designers, and technology experts is asking too much (Huett et al., 2008). Distance education requires collaboration among educators. School librarians are trained and knowledgeable in the use of information technology. Thus, they are important instructional partners who can work with administrators and teachers to help provide resources and services for students enrolling in distance education courses. They are able to provide access to materials in all formats and can help create curricula that will provide engaging learning experiences for students. School librarians can help provide access to materials for distance education students by identifying appropriate resources and their locations, creating bibliographies, developing flexible lending policies, and providing places for interaction such as teleconferencing or group meetings (Schamber, 2004). Administrators should collaborate by making certain that school libraries are provided with up-to-date interactive multimedia equipment, as well as distance learning capabilities (Weil, 2010).

Like some educational trends, distance education is not going away. It is here to stay and will most likely continue to grow rapidly in school districts throughout the United States. It is important that school librarians familiarize themselves with all the distance education programs and courses that are offered in their school districts and be ready to provide the materials and resources needed for lessons and projects in those courses. This requires collaboration, not only with teachers of the distance education courses, but also with other school librarians in the district to make certain that all resources in the district can be shared by distance education students.

Emerging technologies will make many more instructional approaches possible in distance education and will most likely lower the costs and increase interactions between students and teachers. School librarians must continuously stay abreast of all these technologies and the opportunities that they present to their students and teachers.

Conclusions

The number of school districts offering distance education for students is steadily increasing. All indications are that online learning will continue to grow in the future. Like all educational trends, distance education has its pros and cons, but it is a very real presence in today's K–12 schools, and scholars have begun to conduct more research on its characteristics and the factors that impact online education. Although some research has determined characteristics of students and instruction that appear to predict student success in virtual learning, more research about distance education is needed, particularly as it relates to younger students. Collaboration of educators is essential for the success of distance education. School librarians can play an important role in collaboration by assisting teachers with instructional design of their virtual courses and providing the necessary resources and services through technology. School librarians must continue to stay abreast of the concept of distance education and the technologies involved so they can make themselves available experts on distance education.

References

Allen, Elaine, & Seaman, Jeff. (2006). *Making the grade: Online education in the United States.* Needham, MA: Sloan Consortium.

Archambault, Leanna, & Crippen, Kent. (2009). K–12 distance educators at work: Who's teaching online across the United States. *Journal of Research on Technology in Education, 41* (4), 363–391.

Barbour, Michael K., & Reeves, Thomas C. (2009). The reality of virtual schools: A review of the literature. *Computers & Education, 52* (2), 402–416.

Evergreen Education Group. (2009). *Keeping pace with K–12 online learning: An annual review of state-level policy and practice.* Retrieved from http://www.kpk12.com/

Huerta, Luis A., d'Entremont, Chad, & Gonzalez, Maria Fernanda. (2006). Cyber charter schools: Can accountability keep pace with innovation? *Phi Delta Kappan, 88* (1), 23–30.

Huett, Jason, Moller, Leslie, Foshay, Wellesley R., & Coleman, Craig. (2008). The evolution of distance education: Implications for instructional design on the potential of the Web. *TechTrends, 52* (5), 63–67.

International Association for K–12 Online Learning. (n.d.). *Fast facts about online learning.* Retrieved from http://www.inacol.org/press/docs/nacol_fast_facts.pdf

Rice, Kerry Lynn. (2006). A comprehensive look at distance education in the K–12 context. *Journal of Research on Technology in Education, 38* (4), 425–448.

Roblyer, M. D., & Marshall, Jon C. (2002/2003). Predicting success of virtual high school students: Preliminary results from an educational success prediction instrument. *Journal of Research on Technology in Education, 35* (2), 241–255.

Schamber, Linda. (2004). *Distance education and the changing role of the library media specialist.* Retrieved from http://www.libraryinstruction.com/distance-education.html

Schlosser, Lee Ayers, & Simonson, Michael. (2002). *Distance education: Definition and glossary of terms.* Bloomington, IN: Association for Educational Communications and Technology.

Schlosser, Lee Ayers, & Simonson, Michael. (2010). *Distance education: Definition and glossary of terms.* Charlotte, NC: Information Age Publishing.

Sloan Consortium. (2009). *K–12 online learning: A 2008 follow-up of the survey of U.S. school district administrators.* Retrieved from http:// www.sloan-c.org/publications/ survey/pdf/k-12_online_learning_2008.pdf

United States Distance Learning Association. (n.d.). *About us.* Retrieved from http://www. usdla.org/html/aboutUs/vmd.htm

Weil, Eric. (2010). *Meet your new school library media specialist.* Retrieved from http:// www2.scholastic.com/browse/article.jsp?id=3748779

Suggested Activities

1. Interview an instructor of a distance education course. Ask questions relating to the differences between teaching online or in a traditional face-to-face classroom.

2. Enroll in an online course. Write a report on the advantages and disadvantages of being a student in the course. Include some suggestions on how your learning experience could have been improved.

3. Research some of the virtual schools in various states, such as the Arizona Virtual Academy or the Florida Virtual School. In a paper or PowerPoint presentation compare and contrast some of the schools including the types of courses offered, student eligibility, funding, and technical assistance.

4. Interview school librarians who work in a school district where many students enroll in distance education courses. Ask the librarians questions relating to their collaborative efforts to assist with distance education.

CHAPTER **10**

Inclusion

The term *inclusion* generally refers to a movement to educate students with disabilities in a regular classroom setting, along with nondisabled students. In some school districts the term *inclusive* has been broadened to also refer to including all students (not only those with disabilities) in regular classrooms. For instance, this broader concept also includes not separating students out of a regular classroom based on ability, racial background, income, or if the students' first language is not English. The broader concept that sometimes is referred to as *social inclusion* emphasizes a philosophy of establishing classrooms where all students have an authentic sense of belonging.

Although both concepts of inclusion are equally important, this chapter deals with the more popular term that refers to placement of students with disabilities in regular classrooms, where the general education teacher is in charge of all students in the classroom. Even with that definition in mind there are not always clear understandings of the term *inclusion*. Some persons use it interchangeably with the term *mainstreaming*. Mainstreaming, however, is the physical placement of students with disabilities in a regular classroom setting for at least part of a school day. There is not a special emphasis on the achievement of the students with disabilities who are mainstreamed into regular classrooms. Inclusion, on the other hand, refers to accommodating all students in the schools that they would normally attend (neighborhood schools) and seldom, if ever, would students with disabilities be out of regular classrooms. In an inclusive classroom emphasis is placed on educating *all* the children to the greatest extent possible. There is a commitment to move all the needed services and resources to the child with disabilities, rather than moving the child out of the classroom to those services and resources. Inclusion differs from full inclusion in that it allows for other alternative placements of students with disabilities when deemed more appropriate. *Full inclusion* means that all students, regardless of the condition or severity of their disabilities, are in a regular classroom program full-time, and all services are taken to the students in that setting (SEDL, 2010; WEAC, 2007).

Federal Legislation

Two federal laws govern the education of children with disabilities. These two laws do not require inclusion, but they do require that effort be made to find an inclusive placement (WEAC, 2007).

The Individuals with Disabilities Education Act was amended in 2004 and is now known as the Individuals with Disabilities Education Improvement Act of 2004 (P.L. 108–446) or IDEA. This act does not require inclusion, but does require that children with disabilities be educated in "the least restrictive environment" that will meet their individual needs. It also requires school districts to have a continuum of placements available, from the regular classrooms to residential settings, so the needs of all students with disabilities can be met. IDEA states that an individualized education plan (IEP) must be developed for each child with a disability and that the first consideration is to place a child with a disability in a regular classroom. If the IEP team (generally made up of educators, parents, or others with special knowledge about the child) determines that the most appropriate placement is an alternative setting, then the team must include in the child's IEP the reason why a regular classroom setting is not appropriate.

Section 504 of the Rehabilitation Act of 1973 requires that school districts that receive federal funds must provide education for all students with handicaps (language used in the act) and that the handicapped students be placed in regular educational environments unless it is demonstrated that a child's education cannot be achieved satisfactorily in the regular school environment with the use of supplementary aides and services (WEAC, 2007).

In addition to the two federal laws mentioned above, the U.S. Congressional No Child Left Behind Act of 2001 (P.L. 107–110), commonly known as NCLB, also has significant applications to all students with disabilities. The act, which was designed to provide a high-quality education to all students, requires state-by-state accountability systems. These systems must measure and report the academic progress of underserved student population groups, including students with disabilities.

The Educational Policy Reform Research Institute (EPRRI) was established in 2000 and is funded by the U.S. Department of Education. One of EPRRI's objectives is to investigate the impact of educational reform on students with disabilities. The Institute conducts in-depth research at all levels of the education system. Recent research conducted by EPRRI reveals a complex situation in which the educational success of students with disabilities depends on several factors including access to the general curriculum and training educators to teach diverse learners (Nagle, Yunker, & Malmgren, 2006).

Controversy

As with almost any educational reform or trend, there has been controversy about inclusion. During a recent semester, the author of this book asked her class of graduate library science students to discuss the advantages and disadvantages of inclusion. Some of the students were hesitant to mention any disadvantages, stating that doing so might be considered politically incorrect. However, it is important to note that educational trends and reforms have disadvantages, as well as benefits. No educational trend, whether it is standardized tests, block scheduling, or electronic reading programs, is the panacea for educational problems or issues. We should not be hesitant to discuss educational trends and reform. Just as no one method of learning serves perfectly the needs of all students, so, too, an educational trend may not meet the needs of all those involved. With that in mind, the following are some of the arguments that have been provided by both opponents and advocates of inclusion.

Opponents of Inclusion

Many who oppose inclusion point out the difficulty of offering the same quality of education to diverse students who have a wide variety of learning needs and characteristics (Freire, 2009). They feel that students with special needs require teachers who are specially trained in the area of special education. They point out that even the best and most willing teachers have difficulties meeting the needs of the regular students in classrooms, let alone the special requirements of students with moderate and severe disabilities (Dixon, 2005).

In regard to the education of deaf students, inclusion is particularly controversial. Those who oppose inclusion feel that deaf education should take place in sign-bilingual environments, rather than in regular classrooms (Leach & Duffy, 2009).

Another argument is that the psychological demands made on students with disabilities in a regular classroom are not appropriate. Forcing these students to associate with students who have many more capabilities puts undue pressures on the children with disabilities.

Additionally, those who oppose inclusion think that the focus of education for many students with special needs should be on vocational and life skills, rather than the academic skills that are generally emphasized in regular classrooms. Still others fear that the curriculum in the regular classroom will be dumbed down to accommodate the needs of the students with disabilities.

Educators are not the only persons concerned about inclusion. Some parents do not support the approach. They fear that special education services that they have fought for will be lost and that their children will be dumped into regular classrooms without the needed support (Cromwell, 2004). The parents of regular students may be resentful of the attention and extra time given to the children with disabilities and thus these parents may think their children are not receiving the proper amount of education.

According to Berg (2004), those who oppose inclusion have additional concerns about the regular students in the inclusive classroom. They feel that these students are distracted by having extra adults in the room and by having students with disabilities who may cause disruptions. Regular students may resent children with disabilities and tease those students or else act out to get the special attention that teachers appear to be giving to the students with disabilities.

Opponents of inclusion also feel that when inclusion is not implemented appropriately, as sometimes happens, it can have detrimental effects on all involved (Berg, 2004). Teachers who are not properly trained and supported may fear that they will not succeed in carrying out inclusion in their classrooms. It might cause these regular classroom teachers to have negative feelings about their jobs and perhaps even leave the profession. It is also sometimes difficult for general education teachers to have other teachers in their classrooms and to share the control with special education teachers.

Lastly, adversaries of inclusion suspect that school administrations are moving toward more inclusive approaches for budgetary reasons, rather than for what is best for students. Special education in alternative settings tends to be more expensive than inclusive education so opponents of inclusion think this is a consideration that should at least be addressed.

Proponents of Inclusion

Persons who favor inclusion over separate alternative options note numerous advantages of the inclusive approach. Advocates of inclusion feel that students have more sense of belonging in an inclusive classroom, rather than in alternative settings. They argue that inclusion is not just a placement of students into regular classrooms, but it is a philosophy that benefits all students. As Causton-Theoharis and Theorharis (2008) note, "Inclusion is not a place, but rather a way of thinking."

Proponents of inclusion believe that students with disabilities, especially those with autism who experience difficulty with social interactions, benefit by observing and interacting with typical students. Students in an inclusive classroom learn from one another and also learn to respect each others' differences and commonalities (Dixon, 2005).

Labeling students with disabilities as "special" tends to lessen their self-esteem. Often this labeling disappears when these students are placed in inclusive classrooms. Thus, advocates include this as an additional benefit of inclusion.

One of the advantages most often mentioned by proponents of inclusion is that students without particular disabilities develop more accepting attitudes toward disabilities. Having children with disabilities in their classrooms takes away the fear and uneasiness that regular students often feel in regard to their classmates with disabilities (Berg, 2004). If students with disabilities are included in general education classrooms in their neighborhood schools from preschool onward, then their disabilities are simply accepted as a way of life (Dixon, 2005).

Another advantage advocates list is that students with disabilities are able to learn more about realistic life when placed in typical classrooms. The children with disabilities also have opportunities to develop friendships with typically developing peers.

Proponents argue that the education of children with disabilities is more effective by creating higher expectations for such children. They believe that by having access to the general curriculum and exposure to other students in a regular classroom it is possible for students with disabilities to achieve at higher levels.

There are also advantages for regular students when inclusion is used in schools. Regular students can develop important skills, such as leadership, increased abilities to help and teach others, and mentoring, all of which will benefit them in their adult lives.

Advocates of inclusion additionally mention benefits for regular teachers of inclusive classrooms. They believe that inclusion creates an awareness and appreciation of differences in children, as well as helping teachers learn teaching techniques that can help with all their students. Developing teamwork skills is also mentioned as an advantage for both general education and special education teachers (Berg, 2004).

When implemented correctly, proponents of inclusion believe that all students benefit from the rich environments and natural supports that are found in general education classrooms. Although inclusion appears to be the choice of most school districts today, the research on inclusion thus far is inconclusive. Educators who support inclusion, as well as those who resist it, are able to find research to support their views (Nichols, 2008).

Recommendations for Implementing Inclusion

General education teachers are increasingly finding themselves responsible for serving special needs students in regular classrooms. Yet the teachers may not feel that they have the necessary training or support to be successful. The following are some recommendations that can improve the success of inclusive education:

- In a school district the superintendent and each principal must articulate a vision and commitment to the philosophy of inclusion.
- Parents and students should be involved in decision-making processes.
- All placement decisions should be based on well-developed IEPs.
- Explicit training for teachers and staff to build their capacities to support all students in inclusive classrooms must be provided.
- Reduced class sizes and increased numbers of teachers in the classrooms are necessary.
- A licensed classroom teacher and special education teacher need to be placed in each classroom, with support from specialists, such as signers for deaf students.
- Time needs to be provided for regular classroom teachers and special education teachers to collaboratively plan.
- Flexible curricula and instruction need to be established so that all students are working toward the same overall educational outcomes, just with different levels of the outcomes achieved.
- The concerns of school personnel, parents, and students should be monitored and evaluated.
- Ongoing consulting, coaching, and staff development should be provided to teachers.
- The creation and funding of separate spaces for students in a school should be eliminated.
- Sufficient funding based on student need, rather than availability of funds, needs to be assured.

An additional recommendation for dealing with students in inclusive classrooms is utilizing response to intervention (RTI), which is a method of identifying and assisting students who are having difficulty learning. The purpose of RTI is to prevent academic failure through early intervention. RTI uses a multitiered approach to dealing with students who are experiencing academic and behavioral difficulties. The tiered model has three levels:

- **Level 1—Primary:** Data on students' progress is collected. A team discusses research-based interventions to be used by the classroom teacher for students who are having academic difficulty. The teacher provides the interventions, and progress is monitored and reviewed by the team.
- **Level 2—Secondary:** Children who continue to struggle are provided with more intense general education intervention, presumably in small groups.
- **Level 3—Tertiary:** Children who are still experiencing difficulty are placed in special education programs and their functioning is determined by their

individualized education plans (IEPs). Special education teachers deliver the more intense instruction.

Early Intervening Services (EIS) is now mentioned in IDEA, and the act authorizes the use of up to 15 percent of IDEA allocated funds for EIS (James, 2004). Currently, RTI is used primarily for students struggling in reading and mathematics.

The Role of the School Librarian

The school librarian can serve teachers in a school, as well as parents, by providing access to resources that deal with inclusion. Included should be books that can be checked out and a file containing recent articles that discuss inclusion. A bibliography of Web sites, articles, and books should be available and ready to give to any parents, teachers, or administrators seeking information about inclusion. New teachers in a school especially appreciate this assistance. It is important to include reliable sources that explain the federal legislation that applies to students with disabilities. Resources on specific disabilities can be found in many places including the Association of Specialized and Cooperative Library Agencies (ASCLA), a division of the American Library Association, which publishes a few books that deal with disabilities and how to serve persons with disabilities in a library, and the Council for Exceptional Children (CEC), which has a large number of resources which can be purchased through their Web site http://www.cec.sped.org/AM/Template. cfm?Section=Publications1. The availability of resources in the school should be announced in faculty meetings, in school newsletters, and on the school library Web site.

In addition to resources for parents and teachers, the school librarian should provide materials that relate to all students that are included in the Individuals with Disabilities Education Act. Materials should be both fiction and nonfiction, and in print and electronic formats. It is essential that students are able to find materials at their grade level and interest level that reflect an acceptance of their disability or particular need. Terrile (2009) lists the following categories of students receiving services for disabilities in IDEA:

- Mental retardation
- Hearing impairments, including deafness
- Speech or language impairments
- Visual impairments, including blindness
- Emotional disturbances
- Orthopedic impairments
- Autism
- Traumatic brain injury
- Other health impairments
- Multiple disabilities, such as deaf-blindness
- Specific learning disabilities
- Developmental delay

Crystal E. Kaiser (2007) mentions that librarians may have difficulty locating titles of current materials in which children with special needs are represented. Many of the books go out of print quickly because of relatively limited audiences, and many of the titles are available from small, specialty publishing houses that may have limited visibility within mainstream library sources. In an article in the winter 2007 issue of *Children & Libraries*, Kaiser lists more than 300 such titles for children. The titles are listed according to category.

Physical Facility Considerations

To make the school library a welcoming, usable environment for all students, several physical considerations should be addressed. Legislation relating to providing facilities for the physically disabled emphasizes barrier-free environments. School librarians should access the Americans with Disabilities Act (ADA) for physical facility guidelines for libraries. A school librarian can organize the library's physical structure, as well as the resources and services provided, to create the "least restrictive environment" to serve all students in a school.

The library should meet the same standards as other areas of the school. Adaptations that are made to the facility should be a natural part of the school library. Physically challenged students using the library not only need to have an environment where they can be successful, but they also need to be able to learn to function independently.

An ideal entrance to the school library is one in which the physically challenged student can push a large electric button at wheelchair level and automatic doors open. Any doors within the facility should all swing the same way. Doors of unbreakable glass may help some students with visibility or mobility impairments by helping them see what is on the other side of the door. Painting the frame of a door a contrasting color will also help these students locate the door more easily. If a door has a doorknob, some students with weak or uncoordinated hands may have difficulty opening it. Special coverings for doorknobs can be purchased to make the knobs less slippery and easier to turn. Lever types of handles tend to be a better choice as they are easier for physically challenged students to manipulate (Walling & Karrenbrock, 1993).

If there is a change in levels at the entrance or within the library, then a sloping surface or ramp should be provided. If the change in levels is more than one-half inch, then a ramp is required (Walling & Karrenbrock, 1993). If the school library is located on a floor above ground level, then elevator access should be provided. If a security system is in use, it should be barrier-free and not have turnstiles.

Students with visual and mobility impairments need to be able to feel confident that they can move about the library safely. Thus, moving furniture around frequently is not a good idea. Getting rid of any unneeded clutter or small obstacles, such as raised electric outlet covers, will also help keep students from tripping or falling. Textured patterns on the floor covering can help students who are blind or visually impaired know when they are leaving one area and going into another. While smooth, uncarpeted floors might be helpful to students in wheelchairs, students with hearing problems are better served by sound absorbing carpeting. Thus, what might be beneficial for one physically challenged student may not always be the best choice for another student with a different physical disability.

Large pieces of furniture, such as bookcases, can also help students with visual impairments more easily negotiate a traffic pattern. All furniture should be sturdy and stable since children who are physically disabled make heavy use of furniture to help raise and lower their bodies. Some tables need to be high enough for wheelchair arms to slide under, although the size of wheelchairs varies. Tables with semicircular cutouts are helpful to students with mobility handicaps. Chairs that swivel can also be beneficial to students with certain mobility disabilities, especially those students who experience pain with movement.

At least some of the computers in a library need to be at levels where students in wheelchairs are able to work comfortably. Sliding shelves that come out from under a higher table can sometimes serve the purpose if the keyboard is located on the shelf. However, one must take into consideration how far away the monitor is located. Students must be able to use a keyboard and look at the monitor comfortably at the same time.

Bookshelves should be far enough apart for students in wheelchairs to move between the stacks (at least 36 inches for ADA compliance), turn around, and turn their wheelchairs to face the books. Some students may have difficulty reaching items on shelves so providing some type of tool to extend the reach of physically disabled students is a possibility. Heavily used items, such as recreation magazines or newspapers in a high school library, should be shelved on racks that can easily be reached by students in wheelchairs.

Adequate, glare-free lighting is important for all students, but particularly for the visually impaired. Shades and blinds on windows make it possible to adjust lighting for individual needs. Portable reading lamps can also serve the special needs of students with visual disabilities.

Good acoustics in a room are also as important as adequate lighting, especially for students with hearing or speech disabilities. Floor, ceiling, and wall coverings all affect the acoustics of a room, as does the room size and furniture arrangement. Some professional assistance in providing good acoustics may be needed. Providing headphones for the hard of hearing students when they are watching a video or using a computer may also be beneficial.

Excellent signage, including large visual symbols, can be especially helpful to physically challenged students in a school library. Signs with raised letters and/or Braille symbols are ideal. The type fonts on signs should be simple and in contrast with backgrounds. The addition of color coding to signage can provide an extra cue to aid in the location of resources (Guild, 2008). It is especially important that lettering on emergency and directional signs for evacuation exits be large and easy to read. Flashing lights for fire alarms or other alarm indicators will assist the deaf or hearing-impaired students. Having practice emergency drills will help both the physically challenged students and the library staff be prepared for emergency situations.

Numerous studies have attested to the importance of good school libraries for student success. Providing a facility that serves the needs of students with disabilities can help ensure that these students join their fellow classmates in such success.

Collaboration with Special Education and Classroom Teachers

The absence of collaboration between educators in a school has been recognized as a key barrier to successful delivery of services for students with special needs (Murray, 2001). In an inclusive classroom, the role of the classroom teacher may be that of a coach or facilitator, who needs to work with other professionals, teacher aides, and paraprofessionals to serve the needs of all the students in the classroom. School librarians should be included in these collaborations. In order to work collaboratively with special education and classroom teachers, a librarian must be familiar with the IEPs and learning profiles of students with special needs who come to the library. Students with disabilities may need graphic organizers to help complete assignments or they may need structured guidance in planning the steps for a search. A student who has difficulties with spatial orientation may need to be taken directly to resources, rather than be given directions to shelves in order to locate specific materials (Guild, 2008). If working with students with visual disabilities (those who have problems focusing on things), the librarian should get down to their physical level, by either sitting down or squatting. This is also true when talking with students who are in a wheelchair (Vogel, 2008). Knowing the needs of students and how those needs can be met are essential when a school librarian is working collaboratively with students in the library or in an inclusive classroom.

One area in which the school librarian can contribute immensely to the education of students with disabilities is in the acquisition of information literacy skills. It is especially important that these students be able to access information since this will impact their lives. Teaching information skills cooperatively helps learners make transitions from one setting (such as the classroom) to another (such as the school library). It also has another advantage—the librarian becomes one more person with whom students with disabilities can interact, thus increasing their social skills. School librarians can also learn much from special education teachers by watching how they communicate with students with disabilities. For instance, information may be provided to students in small amounts, rather than giving all the information at one time. Many students with disabilities also learn better through auditory or visual stimuli than print material. The school librarian might need to use more multimedia in teaching information skills to these students (Murray, 2001). The librarian may also need to bookmark Web sites for some students, making certain that the sites have clear instructions, have readable text, and are uncluttered. The use of Track Star, http://trackstar.4teachers.org/trackstar/, an online tool, can be used to organize a student's Web search and provide the students with structured learning activities (Juozaitis, 2004).

The research on the successful integration of students with disabilities into classrooms indicates that a school-wide effort is needed, where all personnel in the school are involved in helping students achieve a standards-based education (Juozaitis, 2004). Therefore, it is important that the personnel (both professional and staff) in a school library be a part of this all-important effort.

Assistive Technology

In recent years science has made huge strides in providing technology that can assist persons with a variety of disabilities. One of the principles of librarianship is that information should be accessible to everyone. Many teachers in inclusive classrooms are not fully aware of the technologies that are available to help students with disabilities be successful in their classrooms. Thus, it is important for school librarians to not only have assistive technology (AT) present in their libraries, but also to inform other educators in the school about the availability of these technologies. *Assistive technologies* are defined by the U.S. Technology-Related Assistance for Individuals with Disabilities Act, 1988, (P. L. 100–407) as "any item, piece of equipment or product system, whether acquired commercially, off the shelf, modified, or customized, that is used to increase or improve functional capabilities of individuals with disabilities" (University of Iowa, 2006).

Recently there has also been an emphasis on universal design for learning (UDL), which can support the educational needs of all learners for all students. Gavigan and Kurtts (2009) state, "When educators plan and support instruction using universal design for learning, there is the expectation that a wide range of learning styles and abilities will be served in the classroom."

According to Poel (2007), in the 1970s there were fewer than 100 AT devices available commercially in the United States. Today there are over 29,000 AT devices available for persons with disabilities and aging adults (Simpson, McBride, Spencer, Lowdermilk, & Lynch, 2009). There is a huge range of devices from simple low-tech items, such as pencil grips, spring-loaded scissors, large print books and magazines, a foot mouse for computers, and write-on/wipe off boards to high-powered wheelchairs, pneumatic doors, and sophisticated computer software programs, with screen magnifiers and voice-to-print applications.

SMART Boards, available through SMART Technologies, have become popular in many school libraries and classrooms. A touch-sensitive display on the white board makes it possible for the user to connect directly to a computer-generated projection; thus, the user is able to control the computer display by simply touching the white board screen. SMART Boards are not only useful for teachers and school librarians instructing an entire class, but also can be used for students who cannot directly manipulate a keyboard (Neal & Ehlert, 2006).

In 2008, Follett Destiny released a new visual search feature to their Version 8 Online Public Access Catalog (OPAC). It offers a graphic search and provides alternate term suggestions for misspellings (perhaps due to students with mental or physical challenges). The changes in the OPAC allow students with disabilities to work more independently and to experience more successful searches ("Reorganizing the School Library," 2009).

Progress has also been made in making Web sites more accessible to the physically challenged. In 1999, the World Wide Web Consortium (W3C), which focuses on developing standards for the Web, published the *Web Content Accessibility Guidelines* (WCAG1.0), which has been widely accepted. In December 2008 W3C released an updated version (WCAG2.0). The guidelines are written for a Web technology audience, but school instructional technology professionals can help determine what aspects of the guidelines can be applied to school Web sites. Some accessibility guidelines that can be easily understood and applied include putting all text in a single column, using levels of headings to organize text, avoiding the use of moving or flashing text, using contrasts between text and background colors, avoiding the use of frames, and not making interaction with the user time sensitive.

Not only should the librarian make certain the school library Web site is easily accessible to all students in the school, but the librarian should also be instrumental in advocating that vendors provide products that are accessible to all students. Vendors should be told that this is a priority and it will impact purchasing (Edwards-Johnson, 2009).

Assistive technology can be used with all levels of students with disabilities. With the right types of technology, these students can become more independent and academically successful at their enrolled grade levels (Simpson et al., 2009). School librarians must strive to provide the technology and resources to serve students with special needs, both in the library and in inclusive classrooms.

Conclusions

Inclusion programs vary widely from one school district to another. Although inclusion is not required in any legislation, there is federal legislation that governs the education of students with disabilities. As with many educational reforms there is some controversy about inclusion, with advocates and opponents of inclusion setting forth their views. Thus far, research on inclusion is inconclusive, with both sides of the controversy finding research studies that support their views. School librarians can assist with inclusion by working collaboratively with special education and classroom teachers, providing resources about inclusion and students with special needs, making certain that their school library facilities and programs are friendly to students with disabilities, and acting as school leaders by providing information relating to assistive technology.

References

Berg, Shannon. (2004). *The advantages and disadvantages of the inclusion of students with disabilities into regular education classrooms.* Retrieved from http://www.uwstout. edu/lib/thesis/2005/2005bergs.pdf

Causton-Theoharis, Julie, & Theoharis, George. (2008). *School Administrator, 65* (8), 24–28, 30–31.

Cromwell, Sharon. (2004). *Inclusion: Has it gone too far?* Retrieved from http://www. education-world.com/a_curr/curr034.shmtl

Dixon, Sheryle. (2005). Inclusion—not segregation or integration is where a student with special needs belongs. *Journal of Educational Thought, 39* (1), 33–53.

Edwards-Johnson, Adriana. (2009). Library media specialists and assisted technology. *School Library Media Activities Monthly, 25* (10), 22–24.

Freire, Sofia. (2009). Creating inclusive learning environments: Difficulties and opportunities within the new political ethos. *Journal of Deaf Studies and Deaf Education, 14* (1), 131–135.

Gavigan, Karen, & Kurtts, Stephanie. (2009). AT, UD, and thee: Using assistive technology and universal design for learning in 21st-century media centers. *Library Media Connection, 27* (4), 54–56.

Guild, Sandy. (2008). LD accommodations in the school library: Not just for the specialized school anymore. *Knowledge Quest, 37* (1), 24–29.

James, Fiona. (2004). *Response to intervention in the Individuals with Disabilities Act (IDEA).* Retrieved from http://www.reading.org/downloads/resources/IDEA_RTI_ report.pdf

Juozaitis, Vida. (2004). Serving the needs of our students with LD in the school library. *School Libraries in Canada* (Online), *23* (3).

Kaiser, Crystal E. (2007). Is your early childhood collection disability-inclusive and current? *Children & Libraries, 5* (3), 5–12.

Leach, Diane, & Duffy, Mary Lou. (2009). Supporting students with autism spectrum disorders in inclusive settings. *Intervention in School and Clinic, 45* (1), 31–37.

Murray, Janet. (2001). Teaching information skills to students with disabilities: What works. *School Libraries Worldwide, 7* (2), 1–16.

Nagle, Katherine, Yunker, Carolyn, & Malmgren, Kimber W. (2006). Students with disabilities and accountability reform. *Journal of Disability Policy Studies, 17* (1), 28–39.

Neal, Jerry D., & Ehlert, Dennis. (2006). 20 ways to add technology for students with disabilities to the library or media center. *Intervention in School and Clinic, 42* (2), 119–123.

Nichols, Beverly. (2008). *Improving student achievement: 50 research-based strategies.* Columbus, OH: Linworth.

Poel, Elissa Wolfe. (2007). Enhancing what students can do. *Educational Leadership, 64* (5), 64–66.

Reorganizing the school library: An approach to serving the needs of all students. (2009). *Learning & Media, 37* (4), 24–26.

SEDL (2010). *Inclusion: the pros and cons.* Retrieved from http://www.sedl.org/change/issues/issues43/definition_inclusion.html

Simpson, Cynthia G., McBride, Rebecca, Spencer, Vicky G., Lowdermilk, John, & Lynch, Sharon. (2009). Assistive technology: Supporting learners in inclusive classrooms. *Kappa Delta Pi Record, 45* (4), 172–175.

Terrile, Vikki C. (2009). Technology for every teen @ your library. *Young Adult Library Services, 7* (2), 33–36.

University of Iowa. Iowa Center for Assistive Technology Education and Research. (2006). *Assistive technology glossary.* Retrieved from http://www.education.uiowa.edu/icater/AT_glossary.htm

Vogel, Victoria. (2008). Library outreach to teens with physical challenges. *Young Adult Library Services, 7* (1), 39–42.

Walling, Linda Lucas, & Karrenbrock, Marilyn H. (1993). *The disabled child in the library: Moving into the mainstream.* Englewood, CO: Libraries Unlimited.

WEAC. (2007). *Special education inclusion.* Retrieved from http://www.weac.org/Issues_Advocacy/Resource_Pages_On_Issues_One/Special_Education/special_education_inclusion.aspx

Suggested Activities

1. Research court cases that involve challenges to placement of students in the least restrictive educational environment and report your findings. A few such cases are *Greer v. Rome City School District* (1992), *Sacramento City Unified School District v. Holland* (1994), *Oberti v. Board of Education of the Borough of Clementon School District* (1993), *Poolaw v. Parker Unified School District* (1995), and *School District of Wisconsin Dells v. Z.S.* (2002).

2. Make a bibliography of resources relating to inclusion and provide it to teachers in a school district.

3. Locate and read any research studies dealing with inclusion. Synthesize your findings in a written report.

4. Interview both regular teachers and special education teachers about inclusion. Write interview questions that will address benefits of inclusion, challenges, concerns, and best instructional practices.

Learning More about Educational Trends

This section discussed three educational trends—Web 2.0, distance education, and inclusion. The school librarian can play an important role in these movements when the trends and issues are introduced into a school district or building.

The following are some other educational trends or issues that have implications for the school librarian and the services of the school library program.

- Alternative assessments
- Block scheduling
- Charter schools
- Cooperative learning
- Critical thinking
- Differentiated instruction
- Diversity
- Educational vouchers
- Electronic reading programs
- High-stakes testing programs
- Homeschooling
- Inquiry-based learning
- Integration of technology
- Nongraded schools
- Outcome-based learning
- School-business relationships
- School choice
- School safety
- School-to-work programs
- School uniforms and dress codes
- Service learning
- Site-based management
- Standards and the curriculum

One of the best ways to learn about educational trends or reform movements is to read articles in general education journals, such as *Phi Delta Kappan* or *Education Digest*, as well as in subject specific journals. Frequently, newspaper articles contain discussions relating to specific educational trends, and sometimes television newscasts and public radio broadcasts include information about educational reform movements and issues.

The following are some general Web sites dealing with educational trends and reform. These sites contain links to numerous other sites on specific educational reforms and issues, materials on educational reforms, research related to educational trends, and groups involved in educational reform movements.

The Center for Educational Reform. (2009). *Making schools work better for all children.* Retrieved from http://www.edreform.com/Home/
This site is sponsored by an independent nonprofit organization and provides an overview of school reform issues, news, and research on several reforms.

College of Education, University of Oregon. Clearinghouse on educational policy and management. *Hot topics.* (n.d.). Retrieved from http://eric.uoregon.edu/hot_topics/index.html
> The site contains discussions of several hot topics in education, along with numerous links to other sites that deal with school reforms.

The George Lucas Foundation. (2010). *Edutopia.* Retrieved from http://www.edutopia.org/
> This nonprofit foundation gathers and disseminates innovative models of K–12 teaching and learning. Video clips and blogs, and news are available on the site.

Glossaries of school reform terms can be found in the following resources:

Bermudez, Pedro R., & Lindahl, Lois T. (1999). An evolving list of school reform terms. *Knowledge Quest, 28* (2), 26–30.
> The authors discuss school reform efforts that affect the school culture. Included is a list of defined terms related to the language of educational reform.

National School Reform Faculty. Harmony Education Center. (2008). *Evolving glossary of NSRF terms.* Retrieved from http://www.nsrfharmony.org/glossary.html
> The site notes that an effort has been made to list terms that are in the language of current school reform efforts.

Appendix

Bibliography

Chapter 1—Collaboration and Partnerships

Suggested Readings

Bush, Gail. (2008). Creativity literacy: The library media center as a learning laboratory. *School Library Media Activities Monthly, 24* (6), 24–26.

Buzzeo, Toni. (2008). *The collaboration handbook.* Columbus, OH: Linworth.

Hamilton, Buffy. (2009). Transforming information for NowGen students. *Knowledge Quest, 37* (5), 48–53.

Keeling, Mary. (2009). A district's journey to inquiry. *Knowledge Quest, 38* (2), 32–37.

Kuhlthau, Carol C., Maniotes, Leslie K., & Caspari, Ann K. (2007). *Guided inquiry: Learning in the 21st century.* Westport, CT: Libraries Unlimited.

Ludmer, Robin. (2008). A fixed schedule and successful collaboration—an oxymoron? *School Library Media Activities Monthly, 24* (6), 27–29.

Mardis, Marcia. (2007). Unpacking the baggage of collaboration: Some things to consider. *Media Spectrum, 33* (3), 10–11.

Montiel-Overall, Patricia. (2009). Teachers' perceptions of teacher and librarian collaboration: Instrumentation development and validation. *Library and Information Science Research, 31,* 182–191.

Ogle, Donna. (2009). Creating contexts for inquiry: From KWL to PRC2. *Knowledge Quest, 38* (1), 57–59.

Schultz-Jones, Barbara. (2009). Collaboration in the school social network. *Knowledge Quest, 37* (4), 20–25.

Todd, Ross. (2008). Collaboration: From myth to reality: Let's get down to business. Just do it! *School Library Media Activities, 24* (7), 54–58.

Wolcott, Linda Lachance. (1994). Understanding how teachers plan: Strategies for successful instructional partnerships. *SLMR, 3.* Retrieved from http://www.ala.org/ala/mgrps/divs/aasl/aaslpubsandjournals/slmrb/editorschoiceb/infopower/selctwolcott.cfm

Web Sites

American Association of School Librarians. (2009). *Standards for the 21st-century learner.* Retrieved from http://www.ala.org/ala/mgrps/divs/aasl/guidelinesandstandards/learningstandards/standards.cfm

Funderstanding. (2008). *Constructivism.* Retrieved from http://www.funderstanding.com/content/constructivism

Lamb, Annette, & Johnson, Larry. (2009). *The school library media specialist.* Retrieved from http://eduscapes.com/sms/overview/collaboration.html

Chapter 2—Reading in the Elementary School

Suggested Readings

Anderson, Cynthia. (2009). Five pillars of reading. *Library Media Connection, 28* (2), 22–25.

Duke, Nell K. (2010). The real-world reading and writing U.S. children need. *Phi Delta Kappan, 91* (5), 68–71.

Gordon, Carol A. (2008). A never-ending story: Action research meets summer reading. *Knowledge Quest, 37* (2), 34–41.

Harvey, Carl. (2009). We can open the window to the world. *Knowledge Quest, 37* (5), 26–29.

Joyce, Marilyn Z. (2006). A niche for library media specialists: Teaching students how to read informational texts. *Library Media Connection, 27* (7), 36–38.

Krashen, Stephen. (2009). Anything but reading. *Knowledge Quest, 37* (5), 18–25.

Marcoux, Betty, & Loertscher, David. (2009). The role of a school library in a school's reading program. *Teacher Librarian, 36* (1), 8–14.

Moreillan, Judi. (2009). Reading & the library program: An expanded role for the 21st-century SLMS. *Knowledge Quest, 38* (2), 24–30.

Web Sites

American Association of School Librarians. (2010). *Position statement on the school library media specialist's role in reading.* Retrieved from http://www.ala.org/ala/mgrps/divs/aasl/aaslissues/positionstatements/roleinreading.cfm

American Association of School Librarians. (2010). *School library media specialist's role in reading toolkit.* Retrieved from http://www.ala.org/ala/mgrps/divs/aasl/aaslissues/toolkits/slroleinreading.cfm

International Reading Association. (2003). *Prepared to make a difference: An executive summary of the National Commission on Excellence in Elementary Teacher Preparation for Reading Instruction.* Retrieved from http://www.reading.org/downloads/resources/1061teacher_ed_com_summary.pdf

International Reading Association. (2007). *Teaching reading well: A synthesis of the International Reading Association's research on teacher preparation for reading instruction.* Retrieved from http://www.reading.org/Libraries/SRII/teaching_reading_well.sflb.ashx

International Reading Association. (2010). *Children's choices booklist.* Retrieved from http://www.reading.org/resources/booklists/childrenschoices.aspx

National Council of Teachers of English. (2010). *What do we know about the achievement gap?* Retrieved from http://www.ncte.org/policy-research/wwk/achievementgap

WETA. (2010). *Reading rockets.* Retrieved from http://www.readingrockets.org/

Chapter 3—Music in the Middle School

Suggested Readings

Bush, Jeffrey E. (2001). Composing and arranging in middle school general music. *General Music Today, 21* (1), 6–10.

Eady, Israel, & Wilson, Janell D. (2007). Restructuring music's role in the middle school curriculum. *College Student Journal, 41* (1), 239–241.

Gerber, Timothy, & Gerrity, Kevin. (2007). Principles for principals: Why music remains important in middle schools. *General Music Today, 21* (1), 17–23.

Gerrity, Kevin W. (2009). Enhancing middle-level general music: Suggestions from the literature. *Music Educators Journal, 95* (4), 41–45.

Judah-Lauder, Chris. (2007). Developing young musicians through collaboration. *General Music Today, 21* (1), 11–16.

McAnally, Elizabeth Ann. (2007). Meaningful listening for middle and high school students. *Teaching Music, 15* (1), 22–26.

Van Weelden, Kimberly. (2007). Music for the forgotten: Creating a secondary general music experience for students with special needs. *General Music Today, 21* (1), 26–29.

Web Sites

Bertland, Linda. (n.d.). *Virtual middle school library.* Retrieved from http://www.sldirectory.com/studf/art.html

Children's Music Workshop. (2009). *Music education online.* Retrieved from http://www.childrensmusicworkshop.com/

Education World. (2010). *Making the case for music education.* Retrieved from http://www.educationworld.com/a_curr/curr123.shtml

Estrella, Espie. (2010). *Music education lesson plans.* Retrieved from http://musiced.about.com/od/lessonsandtips/a/lessonbysubject.htm

National Association for Music Education. (2010). *National standards for music education.* Retrieved from http://www.menc.org/resources/view/national-standards-for-music-education

Chapter 4—English as a Second Language in the High School

Suggested Readings

Amsbury, Dawn. (2008). Talking the talk: Library classroom communication and international students. *The Journal of Academic Librarianship, 34* (4), 354–357.

Arsenault, Rochelle & Brown, Penny. (2007). The case for inclusive multicultural collections in the school library. *CSLA Journal, 31* (1), 20–21.

Bordonaro, Karen. (2006). Language learning in the library: An exploratory study of ESL students. *The Journal of Academic Librarianship, 32* (5), 518–526.

Carrigan, Richard P. (2009). Implementing language acquisition in classrooms. *Education Digest, 75* (4), 57–61.

Conteh-Morgan, Miriam. (2002). Connecting the dots: Limited English proficiency, second language learning theories, and information literacy instruction. *The Journal of Academic Librarianship, 28* (4), 191–196.

Dong, Yu Ren. (2005). Getting at the content. *Educational Leadership, 62* (4), 14–19.

Goldsmith, Francisca. (2002). Earphone English. *School Library Journal, 48* (5), 50–53.

Lee, Rebecca. (2006). Effective learning outcomes of ESL elementary and secondary students utilizing educational technology infused with constructivist pedagogy. *International Journal of Instructional Media, 33* (1), 87–93.

Naidoo, Jamie Campbell. (2005). Informational empowerment: Using informational books to connect the library media program with sheltered instruction. *School Libraries Worldwide, 11* (2), 132–152.

Web Sites

Education Commission of the States. (2010). *Bilingual/ESL: What states are doing.* Retrieved from http://www.ecs.org/html/IssueSection.asp?issueid=16&s=What+States+Are+Doing

ESL Globe (2009). *Resources.* Retrieved from http://www.ncsu.edu/eslglobe/globeresourc.html

Office of English Language Acquisition. *Welcome to OELA's home page.* Retrieved from http://www2.ed.gov/about/offices/list/oela/index.html

O'Loughlin, Judith & Haynes, Judie. (2004). Organizing and assessing in the content area class. Retrieved from http://www.everythingesl.net/inservices/judith2.php

Teachers Network.org. (n.d.). *ESL.* Retrieved from http://www.teachersnetwork.org/Teachnet/esl.cfm

Chapter 5—Students Who Are Autistic

Suggested Readings

Banda, Deventer R., Grimmett, Eric, & Hart, Stephanie. (2009). Activity schedules: Helping students with autism spectrum disorders in general education classes manage transitions. *Teaching Exceptional Children, 41* (4), 16–21.

Bloomquist, Shannon. (2005). Autism resources for public libraries: Issues, challenges, and recommended resources. *Indiana Libraries, 24* (3), 23–31.

Chandler-Olcott, Kelly & Kluth, Paula. (2009). Why everyone benefits from including students with autism in literacy classrooms. *Reading Teacher, 62* (7), 548–557.

Farmer, Lesley, & Syles, Maureen. (2008). Library services for students with autism. *CSLA Journal, 31* (2), 25–27.

Friedlander, Diana. (2009). Sam comes to school: Including students with autism in your classroom. *The Clearing House, 82* (3), 141–144.

Roberts, Jacqueline M. A., Keane, Elaine, & Clark, Trevor R. (2008). Making inclusion work. *Teaching Exceptional Children, 41* (2), 22–27.

Whelan, Deborah. (2009). The equal opportunity disorder. *School Library Journal, 55* (8), 30–34.

Web Sites

Abramson, Larry. (2007). *Public schools prepare to educate kids with autism.* Retrieved from http://www.npr.org/templates/story/story.php?storyId=12776434

Autism Society of America. (2008). *About autism.* Retrieved from http://www.autism-society.org/site/PageServer?pagename=about_home

Becker, Jody. (2009). *Behind the autistic statistics.* Retrieved from http://www.theatlantic.com/doc/200910u/autism-diagnoses

Rudy, Lisa Jo. (2009). *Educational options for children with autism.* Retrieved from http://autism.about.com/od/schoolandsummer/a/edoptionshub.htm

Winerman, Lea. (2004). *Effective education for autism*. Retrieved from http://www.apa.org/monitor/dec04/autism.aspx

Chapter 6—Highly Mobile Students

Suggested Readings

Hardy, Lawrence. (2009). The changing face of homelessness. *American School Board Journal, 196* (6), 18–20.

Hartman, Chester. (2006). Students on the move. *Educational Leadership, 63* (5), 20–24.

Matheis, Nancy. (2009). Mobility matters. *Leadership Compass, 6* (4), 1–2.

Rhodes, Virginia L. (2008). Learning on the go: Voices of highly mobile urban students. *Learning Inquiry, 2* (2), 113–125.

Smith, Jean Louise M., Fien, Hank, & Paine, Stan C. (2008). When mobility disrupts learning. *Educational Leadership, 65* (7), 59–63.

Titus, Dale N. (2007). Strategies and resources for enhancing the achievement of mobile students. *NASSP Bulletin, 91* (1), 81–97.

Walker-Dalhouse, Doris, & Risko, Victoria J. (2008). *Reading Teacher, 62* (1), 84–86.

Web Sites

Department of Defense Education Activity. (2009). *Military K–12 partners*. Retrieved from http://militaryk12partners.dodea.edu

Education World. (2010). *Meeting the educational needs of migrant children*. Retrieved from http://www.educationworld.com/a_curr/curr347.shtml

Lips, Dan. (2007). *Foster care children need better educational opportunities*. Retrieved from http://heritage.org/research/education/bg2039.cfm

National Association for the Education of Homeless Children and Youth. (2009). *New from NAEHCY*. Retrieved from http://www.naehcy.org/

National Center for Homeless Education at the Serve Center. (n.d.). *Homeless education issue briefs*. Retrieved from http://www.serve.org/NCHE/briefs.php

Chapter 7—Students with Gay, Lesbian, Bisexual, or Transgender Orientations

Suggested Readings

Chick, Kay. (2008). Fostering an appreciation for all kinds of families: Picturebooks with gay and lesbian themes. *Bookbird, 46* (1), 15–22.

Curwood, Jen Scott, Schliesman, Megan, & Horning, Kathleen T. (2009). Fight for your right: Censorship, selection, and LGBT literature. *English Journal, 98* (4), 37–43.

Gardes, Tim. (2008). Serving lesbian, gay, bisexual, transgendered, and questioning teens in your library media center. *CSLA Journal, 32* (1), 23–24.

Hartman, Karen. (2009). Reading and writing about real issues. *English Journal, 98* (4), 12–13.

Jennings, Kevin. (2006). Librarians make a difference. *Knowledge Quest, 34* (5), 22.

Roeck, Kathryn. (2008). Exploring how to change stereotypical attitudes toward students who are LGBT. *Democracy & Education, 18* (1), 53–56.

Savage, Todd A., & Harley, Debra A. (2009). A place at the blackboard LGBTIQ. *Multicultural Education, 16* (4), 2–9.

Whelan, Debra Lau. (2006). Out and ignored: Why are so many school libraries reluctant to embrace gay teens? *School Library Journal, 52* (1), 46–50.

Young, Sara Lewis-Bernstein. (2009). Breaking the silence: Critical literacy and social action. *English Journal, 98* (4), 109–115.

Web Sites

American Civil Liberties Union. (n.d.). *LGBT rights*. Retrieved from http://www.aclu.org/lgbt-rights

American Library Association. (2009). *The Rainbow Project*. Retrieved from http://www.ala.org/ala/mgrps/rts/glbtrt/rainbow/index.cfm

Cooperative Children's Book Center. (n.d.). *Gay and lesbian themes and topics in selected children's and young adult books*. Retrieved from /www.education.wisc.edu/ccbc/books/detailListBooks.asp?idBookLists=446

GLSEN. (2010). *About us*. Retrieved from http://www.glsen.org/cgi-bin/iowa/all/about/index.html

LAMBDA. (2007). *LAMBDA community services*. Retrieved from http://www.lambda.org/

Pearson, Chris. (2010). *LGBT book reviews for children and young adults*. Retrieved from http://rainbowbooks.wordpress.com/

Chapter 8—Web 2.0

Suggested Readings

Knobel, Michele, & Wilber, Dana. (2009). Let's talk 2.0. *Educational Leadership, 66* (6), 20–24.

Nevin, Roger. (2009). Supporting 21st century learning through Google Apps. *Teacher Librarian, 37* (2), 35–38.

Ohler, Jason. (2009). Orchestrating the media collage. *Educational Leadership, 66* (6), 8–13.

Perez, Lisa. (2009). Using "Second Life" in school librarianship. *Teacher Librarian, 37* (2), 43–44.

Simkins, Michael, & Schultz, Randy. (2010). Using Web 2.0 tools at school. *Leadership, 39* (3), 12–14, 38.

Villano, Matt. (2008). What are we protecting them from? *T.H.E. Journal, 35* (5), 48–50, 52, 54.

Weigel, Margaret, & Gardner, Howard. (2009). The best of both literacies. *Educational Leadership, 66* (6), 38–41.

Web Sites

Bertland, Linda. (n.d.). *Resources for school librarians. Web 2.0 in school libraries*. Retrieved from http://www.sldirectory.com/libsf/resf/web2.html

Center for Safe and Responsible Internet Use. (2010). *Welcome to CSRIU.* Retrieved from http://www.cyberbully.org/

Consortium for School Networking. (n.d.). *CoSN Initiatives.* Retrieved from http://www.cosn.org/Initiatives/tabid/4204/Default.aspx

Davidson, Cathy N. & Goldberg David Theo. (2009). *The future of learning institutions in a digital age.* Retrieved from http://mitpress.mit.edu/books/chapters/Future_of_Learning.pdf

New Media Consortium. (2010). *The 2010 horizon report K—12 edition.* Retrieved from http://www.nmc.org/pdf/2010-Horizon-Report.pdf

Schrock, Kathy. (2010). *Kathy Schrock's guide for educators.* Retrieved from http://school.discoveryeducation.com/schrockguide/edtools.html

YALSA. (2009). *Web 2.0 & libraries.* Retrieved from http://wikis.ala.org/yalsa/index.php/Web_2.0_%26_Libraries

Chapter 9—Distance Education

Suggested Readings

Archambault, Leanna, & Crippen, Kent. (2009). K–12 distance educators at work: Who's teaching online across the United States. *Journal of Research on Technology in Education, 41* (4), 363–391.

Davis, Niki E., & Roblyer, M. D. (2005). Preparing teachers for the "schools that technology built": Evaluation of a program to train teachers for virtual schooling. *Journal of Research on Technology in Education, 37* (4), 399–409.

Kachel, Deborah E., Henry, Nancy L., Keller, Cynthia A. (2005). Making it real online: Distance learning for high school students. *Knowledge Quest, 34* (1), 14–17.

Rice, Kerry Lynn. (2006). A comprehensive look at distance education in the K–12 context. *Journal of Research on Technology in Education, 38* (4), 425–448.

Southwick, J. Wanless. (2003). Distance education in the rural K–12 environment. *Computers in the schools, 20* (3), 27–32.

Web Sites

International Association for K–12 Online Learning. (2006). *National standards of quality for online courses.* Retrieved from http://www.inacol.org/research/nationalstandards

Learning Point Associates. (2008). *Keeping pace with K–12 online learning: A review of state-level policy and practices.* Retrieved from http://www2.learningpt.org/catalog/item.asp?SessionID=369885214&productID=143

PBS Teachers. (n.d.). *Technology integration.* Retrieved from http://www.pbs.org/teachers/librarymedia/tech-integration/

Sloan Consortium. (n.d.). *Welcome to the Sloan Consortium.* Retrieved from http://www.sloan-c.org/

University of Wisconsin-Extension. (2010). *District education clearinghouse.* Retrieved from http://www.uwex.edu/disted/k12.cfm

Chapter 10—Inclusion

Suggested Readings

Alexander, Linda Baldwin. (2005). ADA resources for the library and information professions. *Journal of Education for Library and Information Science, 46* (3), 248–257.

Causton-Theoharis, Julie, & Theoharis, George. (2009). *The Education Digest, 74* (6), 43–47.

Dixon, Sheryle. (2005). Inclusion—not segregation or integration is where a student with disabilities belongs. *Journal of Educational Thought, 39* (1), 33–53.

Edwards-Johnson, Adriana. (2009). Library media specialists and assisted technology. *School Library Media Activities Monthly, 25* (10), 22–24.

Hopkins, Janet. (2004). *Assistive technology: An introductory guide for K–12 library media specialists.* Worthington, OH: Linworth.

Hopkins, Janet. (2005). Extending inclusive learning: Library and special education collaboration. *Library Media Connection, 23* (6), 17–19.

Jones, Jamie L., Zambone, Alana M., Canter-Smith, Lora Lee, & Voytecki, Karen. (2010). The forgotten partners in special education: Teacher-librarians. *Teacher Librarian, 37,* (4), 65–69.

Kozik, Peter L., Cooney, Bernard, Vinciguerra, Scott, Gradel, Kathleen, & Black, Joan. (2009). Promoting inclusion in secondary schools through appreciative inquiry. *American Secondary Education, 38* (1), 77–91.

Neal, Jerry D., & Ehlert, Dennis. (2006). 20 ways to add technology for students with disabilities to the library or media center. *Intervention in School and Clinic, 42* (2), 119–123.

Niesyn, Mary E. (2009). Strategies for success: Evidence-based instructional practices for students with emotional and behavioral disorders. *Preventing School Failure, 53* (4), 227–233.

Web Sites

IncludingAllKids.org. (2010). *What is inclusion?* Retrieved from http://www.includingallkids.org/what-is-inclusion.php

Inclusion Network. (n.d.). *What is inclusion?* Retrieved from http://www.inclusion.com/inclusion.html

National Center for Educational Statistics. (2010). *NAEP inclusion policy.* Retrieved from http://nces.ed.gov/nationsreportcard/about/inclusion.asp

Teacher Vision. (2010). *Special needs—teacher resources.* Retrieved from http://www.teachervision.fen.com/special-education/teacher-resources/6640.html

Index